coalfaces

life after coal in the afan valley

coalfaces

life after coal in the afan valley

tina carr & annemarie schöne

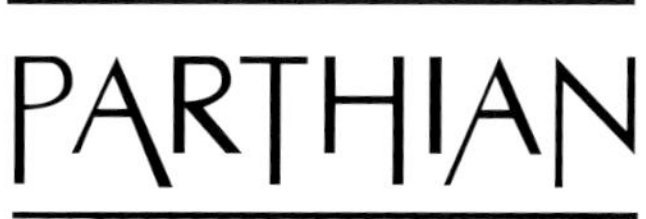

PARTHIAN

Parthian
The Old Surgery
Napier Street
Cardigan
SA43 1ED

www.parthianbooks.co.uk

First published in 2008
© Tina Carr & Annemarie Schöne 2008
Reprinted in a limited edition of 500 July 2024
All Rights Reserved

Edited by Jeff Teare

ISBN 978-1-917140-64-5

Designed and typeset by Lucy Llewellyn

Printed and bound by Gomer, Llandysul, Wales.
Printed using environmentally friendly paper and ink.

The publisher acknowledges the financial support of the Books Council
of Wales.

British Library Cataloguing in Publication Data

A cataloguing record for this book is available from the British Library.

'Work that produces unnecessary consumer junk or weapons of war is wrong and wasteful. Work that is built upon false needs of unbecoming appetites is wrong and wasteful. Work that deceives or manipulates, that exploits or degrades is wrong and wasteful. Work that wounds the environment or makes the world ugly is wrong and wasteful. There is no way to redeem such work by enriching it or restructuring it, by socialising it or nationalising it, by making it "small" or decentralised or democratic.'

Theodore Roszak – cultural historian

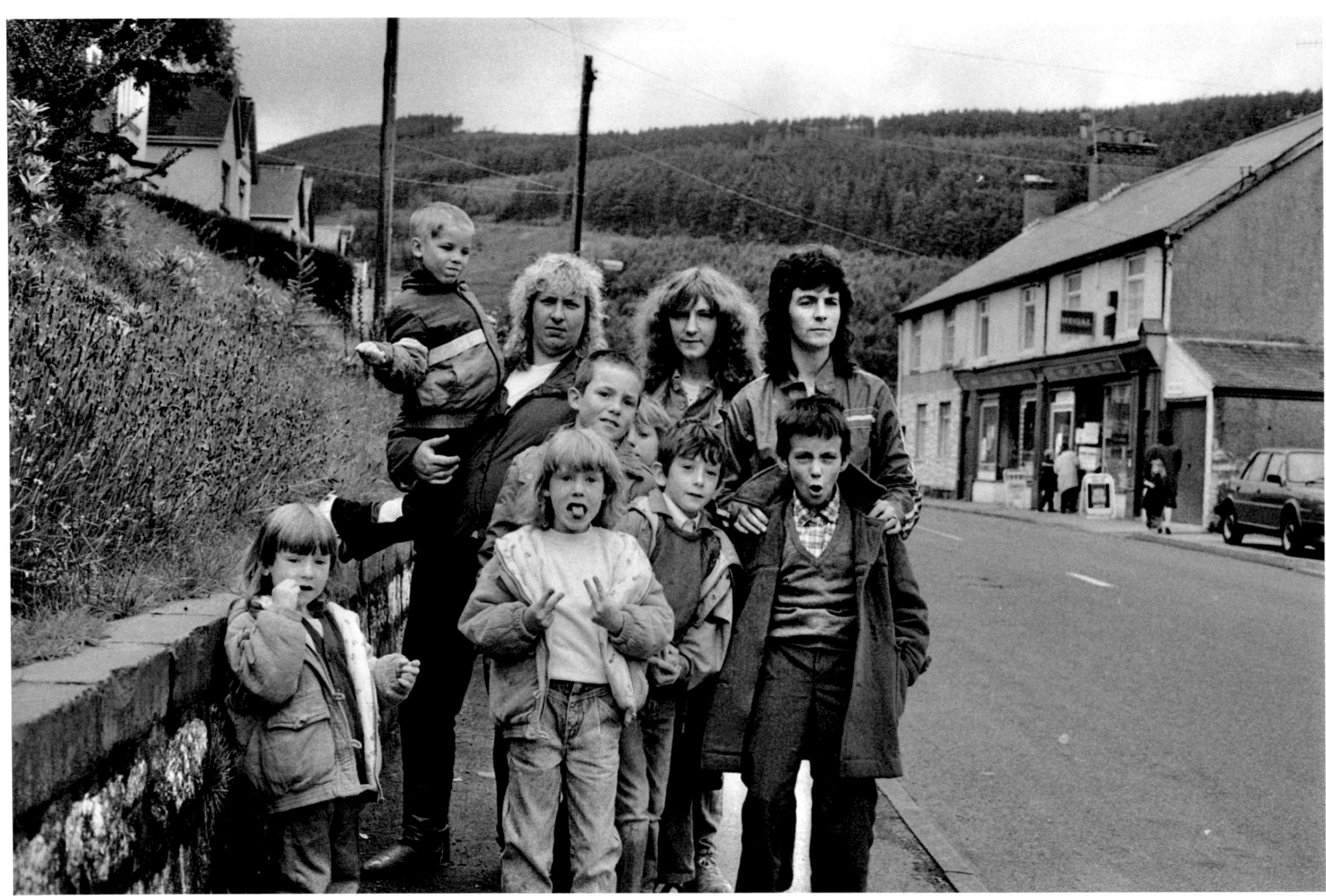

Preface

Dr. Bronwen Colquhoun

I first encountered Tina Carr and Annemarie Schöne's work in November 2021. They had heard that National Museum Wales was actively collecting photographs following the appointment of its first photography curator in 2016, and they contacted me directly to find out more.

I responded to the email immediately, excited by the prospect of learning about two women artists whose work I was somehow unfamiliar with. From their thirty years of living and working in Wales, Carr and Schöne had amassed a substantial archive of photographs that included several major bodies of work. The archive needed a home.

We first met in Carmarthen where I was shown selected photographs from each project. I was immediately captivated by *Coalfaces*. It was vivid, nostalgic, joyful, melancholic and evocative in equal measure. I learned about its significance as the first socially engaged photographic project that had taken place in the south Wales valleys, in which the communities themselves were active collaborators. Its primary aim was to give voice to those communities and empower them to creatively express themselves in the face of societal neglect.

How had I not heard of these artists and of this work before? And how can such a project be marginalised from the story of photography and the south Wales valleys?

Following the visit, we set about acquiring a set of twenty-one framed C-type prints from the series for the permanent collection. With the generous support of Art Fund, the acquisition was completed in early 2024. Simultaneously, the museum was preparing for its first major survey show about the visual culture of the south Wales valleys. *Coalfaces* was to take centre-stage in the exhibition, hanging in the first gallery to introduce and illustrate the core focus of the exhibition; community.

It is no surprise then that since *The Valleys* exhibition opened, *Coalfaces* has captivated both audiences and museum staff. A number of subjects in the photographs have been identified, and anecdotal visitor comments suggest that the work resonates so strongly because of the universality of community and its relationship to place.

It is rare for a photographic project to have such an immediate and powerful impact, and it is such a joy to observe this in the gallery space. *Coalfaces* now has a home, and alongside the archive of the project which Carr and Schöne generously donated, we are committed to sharing this significant work as widely as possible for many, many years to come.

June 2024

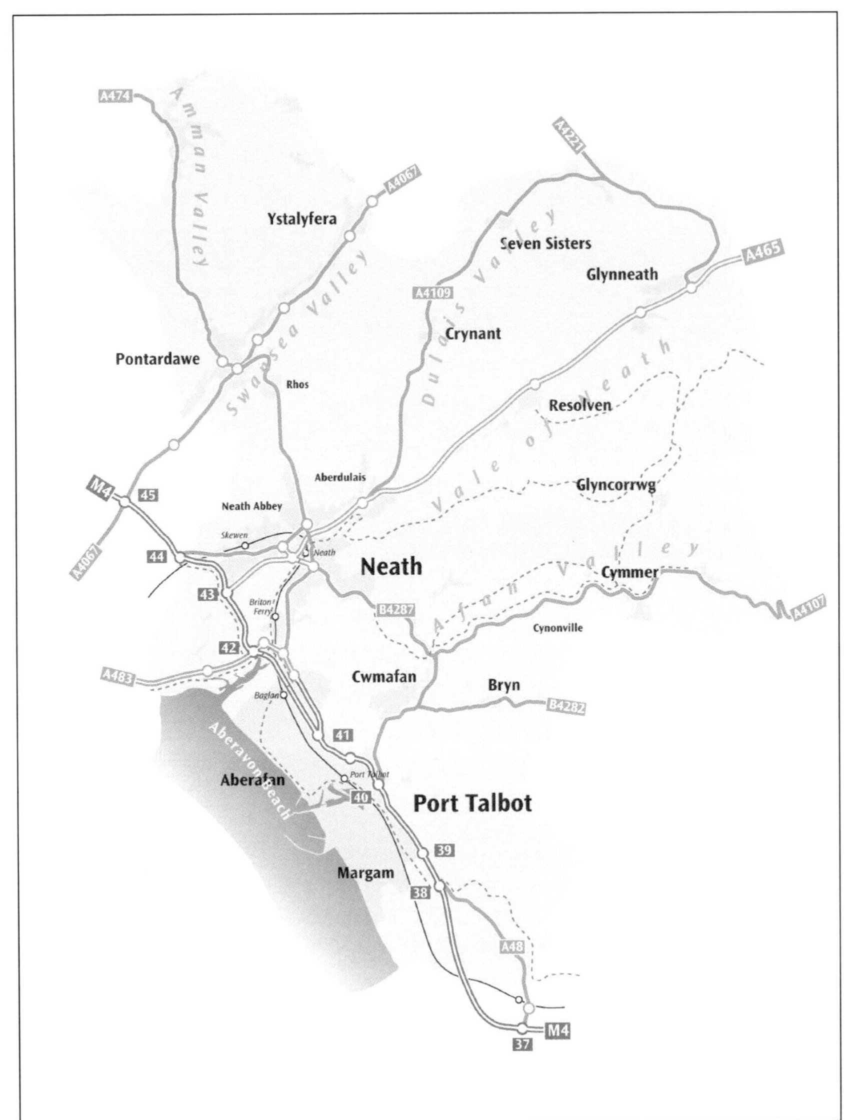

The Afan Valley

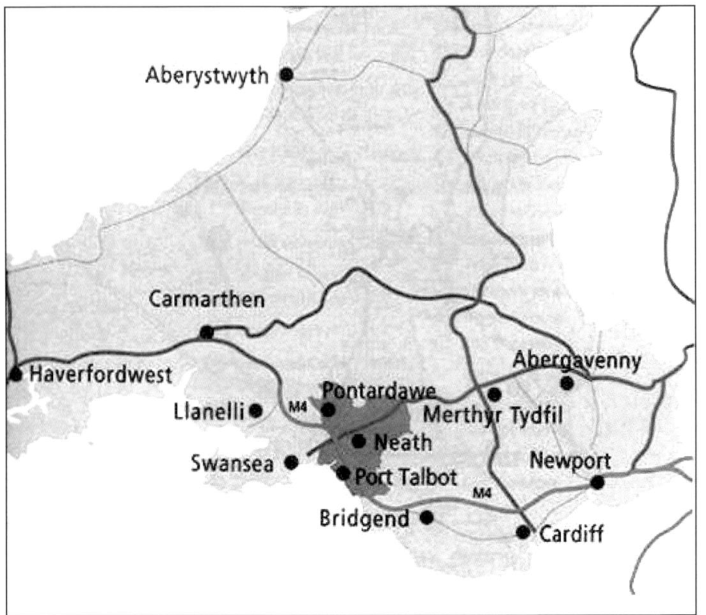

South Wales

contents

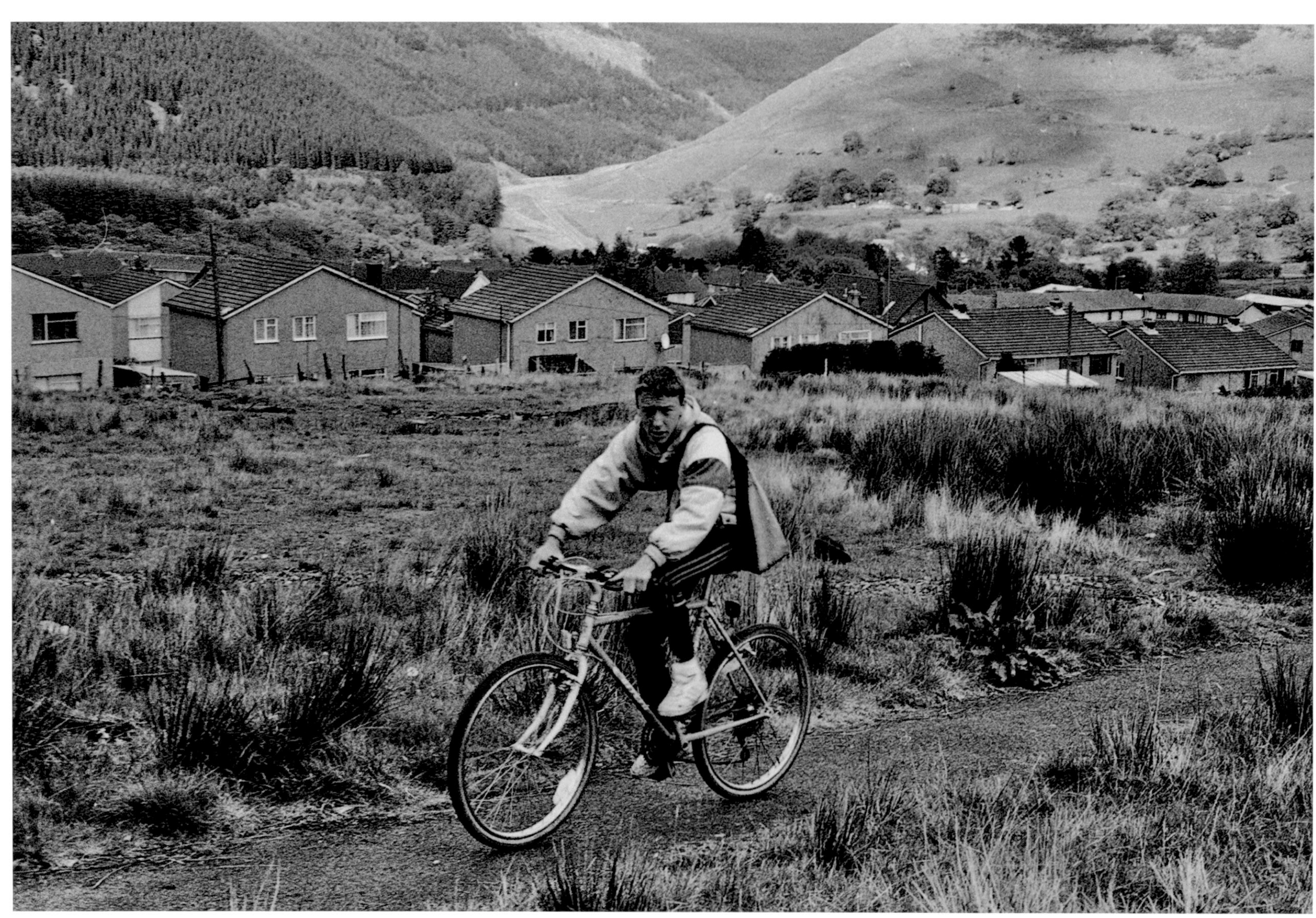

Foreword

Amanda Hopkinson

Tina and Annemarie's work is, above all, about commitment. From 1980, when they first collaborated on the photo-project *River Tyne, from Sources to Mouth*, to 2007, when their exhibition of images of derelict sites in rural west Wales, Abandoned, toured Britain, they have combined working together with a strong sense of responsibility to both place and people.

This is, of course, a photojournalistic tradition with long, strong roots reaching back at least a half-century. Roy Stryker's foundation of the Farm Security Administration in the United States, the involvement of women photographers (often working collaboratively), and the iconic portraits of Dorothea Lange and Walker Evans are a part of that history. It in turn draws on the social consciousness of earlier documentary work by the likes of Jacob Riis, in recording the immigrant-crowded slums of New York of the early twentieth century: not, perhaps, in either concept or sentiment, a million miles away from a project entitled *Brent, the Eighth Most Deprived Borough in the Country*, undertaken by Tina and Annemarie with the support of the former Greater London Council and Brent Trades Council in 1984.

The significance of such a tradition, even when the format alters – large scale C-prints are reproduced in colour – lies in the relationship between photographer and subject. Just as Atget intimately knew (in some sense, as the French have it, visually caressed) the object of his attention, Tina and Annemarie only focus their lens, video or camera, on matters of which they have the most intimate understanding. Where human subjects are involved, then so is trust: it is clear that Tina and Annemarie's subjects are not only volunteers but also collaborators. Trust breeds respectful intimacy but also creative interactivity.

It is not happenstance that projects have titles such as *Same Street as Us*, referencing the place where they formerly lived in Fulham, west London, or that both their major Welsh projects, *Pigs and Ingots* and *Coalfaces*, have been acquired as true records by the National Library of Wales. The principal difference is that the earlier work reads as a microcosm of what was to come: what took two years and one street to produce in the 1980s has given way to work that follows social change across decades and takes in sprawled communities. What remains the same is the fervent attention to detail and the shared responsibility for the work, with each other, and with their human subjects.

In the early eighties Tina and Annemarie moved to Wales. Twenty-five years on it is their world: it encompasses home and work and leisure and nature – and politics. Thatcher's policies of selective de-industrialisation literally changed the face of Britain, city and country alike, forever. Yet there was something over and above the land that has always informed the historically altered landscapes of Tina and Annemarie. The ever-changing western skies, clouds with their chasing shadows, offer a different drama, as expertly lit as any stage set. A preference for natural light and colour imagery, an alternation of found with staged compositions, paradoxically create a sense of hyper-reality, of multiple truths.

What Tina and Anne-Marie have documented are the devastating, long term effects of the previous twenty years of pit closures in one small valley of the South Wales Coalfield; from the mountains, once honeycombed with mines, to the villages, now with bricked up doorways and derelict buildings; from the men 'made redundant' to the women, suddenly become main breadwinners in families forced to live not on the wages of the naturally male 'aristocracy of labour' but on those of traditionally poorly-valued 'women's work'. The Miners' Club gets boarded up, but then so do newer barren concrete substitutes. In fact there's a considerable dearth of glass in the region's windows and doors, always an indicator of local levels of disaffection or identification between residents and their environment. Attempts at conversion evoke a sense of despair alongside the desolation.

What the state calls the 'Employment Office'

and the photographers' caption the 'Unemployment Office' is a former church hall (built 1936) at Cymmer. Past all use, the building is partly overgrown, partly tumbled-down, a testament to the failure to afford salvation in this world or the next. A modern concrete church offers slight alternative: already covered in damp stains and graffiti, predictably windowless. The vicar poses outside with careful bravado: dressed in regulation black; fingers stuck in tight hip pockets; shined shoes; cowlick hair – and only a downcast half-smile to hint how shy he might be without his attitude.

In a series worthy of August Sander, individuals pose with their symbols, as surely as members of any medieval guild. Many of the emblems indeed relate to long before the Industrial Revolutions: the pigeon fancier, holding his feathery bundle; or the whinberry pickers at the base of a stack of shale on which the plants have taken root, displaying their harvest. Animals abound, with only one pony featured in the image called 'Sunnyside Terrace', but plenty of dogs, one being trained by young Robert with shepherd's crook in hand and 'Freeway' being gently patted on the head whilst taking a walk on the industrial estate.

Beyond pit pony and Shank's' pony, transport predominantly comes on two wheels. The school gardener, his features a russet shadow obscured beneath his pull-down hat, cycles to work on a bone-shaker with upswung handlebars, scooting to a halt between the bean-canes and a polytunnel. Teenage motorcyclists swing into view on a low-slung DT rider, shiny red paintwork that perfectly sets off Hugh in black and Jason in white. They're the lucky ones: Italjet Junior Motorcycles has

clearly gone out of business, and a defiant line-up of four smiling guys representing three generations of Valley men (including the possible Italian, in a jaunty trilby, and one more shaggy dog) are flanked by an aged Reliant Robin and a learner Mini. Abandoned cars abound, as do disused railway lines and overgrown roads.

Some images focus in on detail: an artificial pond on which two white ducks paddle unconcerned as a flight of stone steps crumble into the litter-polluted water beneath a row of allotment shacks, also in decline. In the middle distance there is a Park Lane foregrounded by another river crammed with junked rubbish, a row of pink blocks of flats, the ground floor windows routinely caged in. In a deliberate pairing, an abandoned 'Council House' precedes the image of a 'Private House', all stone cladding and plastic garden furniture, fake Grecian urns and lawn gnomes, watched over by Barbara, artfully colour-harmonised and arranged on her swingseat.

Those who assemble in groups tend to be the young – from the mothers' and toddlers' group crowded onto a rubber mat for a group pose to the teenagers huddled in a blind doorway at the bottom of Gwynfi Street. Defiance comes with a 'Children's Camp' who form an ad hoc human pyramid, from which a salvaged steering wheel lends a surreal compass to their human pile. A pool hall and a boxing ring offer transient escapism while pubs with names like 'The Refresh' appear more as waiting rooms, where pints are no longer lined up on the bar but are individually and slowly consumed by men with too much time, and women and children also find their place.

What at first appear as belonging to another genre, that of site-specific large format landscapes, are oddly inhabited. Inhabited less by the living than by absent presences. The theme of post-industrial archaeology is a rich one to mine: since prehistoric times, man has been excavating, eviscerating, exhausting the countryside from within. There is no longer any such thing as a 'natural' landscape: all is man-made – or man-destroyed. Yet it takes remarkably little time, once man again departs, for nature to repossess and replenish, to set about crumbling away and covering over human traces.

Ghosts of those who have lived and worked and multiplied – and, in the space of a generation, been forced to abandon – these small communities have been present in two major bodies of work already achieved by Tina and Annemarie.

In *Pigs and Ingots: The Lead/Silver Mines of Cardiganshire* (1993), time renders the unnatural a part of nature in flooded valleys, dammed lakes, manmade walls of slate and warrens of stone and wood, so well embedded as to be almost indecipherable except from the air, a landscape in continual manipulated evolution across the centuries. Alternating colour and black-and-white images bring the dead matter of metallurgy to life with work that is as much social history as it is bucolic landscapes.

In *Abandoned* (2007), the homes of those who have left their communities also leave a trove of social history behind. These reveal far more than their obsessive possessions (from accumulations of old television sets or margarine cartons to angelic icons and hunting trophies) in terms of a transient social imprint. A recent London showing evoked the description 'medievalist' for its wealth of associative symbols, and Annemarie refers to her love of the Middle Ages for its naïf artists, its hand-illustrated Books of Hours. There is certainly something of that meticulous attention to creative detail. The use of a palette where certain hues predominate: a Welsh affection for turquoise paint-work and pink interiors, for example, or for green and yellow knitwear, remembering the jewelled colours of illuminated borders.

Both Annemarie and Tina are forever 'foreign': the one born and raised in Bavaria, the other in England. Yet in photographic terms, their work brings to mind that of two other famous 'incomers' to their adoptive homeland. Interestingly, both are known for their work in black-and-white, and both for being formed in a reportage tradition.

Magnum photographer David Hurn shares their status as witness, with its connection to being a lifelong outsider. This despite having made Wales his home for over fifty years, much of it devoted to a comprehensive documentation of the country for the National Museum of Wales (shown and toured from the millennium). How-ever it is Edith Tudor Hart (nee Suschitzky), whom the photographers here own as a major source of inspiration. Her particular combination of artistic perfectionism with political activism (she, and her husband, who worked as a GP in the mining communities, were both members of the Communist Party in the 1930s and 1940s) gave rise to a seminal collection of images, published only in the 1980s. The portrait of the unemployed young miner playing his violin or the barefoot children huddled by slagheaps epitomise a very different epoch during an earlier economic Depression. Captions such as No Home, No Dole and Unemployed Miners underline the heart-tearing images.

Yet her commitment and concern are at one with that of Tina and Annemarie, despite the different formal interpretations given to 'human-itarian photography', a tradition that was born with the medium itself but which has been re-invented with every generation who have made it their own. Tudor Hart's book title, chosen by her brother, fel-low photographer and film-maker Wolf Suschitzky, could not have been more appropriate: *The Eye of Conscience* – emphatically not the objective Eye of the Camera but of an artist who refuses to turn a blind eye.

The fear is always that if left unrecorded, a world will vanish forever. Yet it is never enough for a photographer to record: she must also read the material she is working with. There is no such thing as a neutral witness, for no-one can delete personal subjectivity. On the contrary, it is the subjectivity of the photographer that makes the photograph.

The age-old argument over whether the camera can lie can be swiftly settled. Of course the camera cannot lie, but nor can it tell the truth. Unless, that is, it is so directed by the photographer. The truth, a contemporary reality as perceived in all its trans-formations and manifestations, is the stuff of Tina and Annemarie's work. In an age of celebrity and triviality, it shines as a re-valuing of the human spirit: the spirit of those who actively collaborated on *Coalfaces* and of the photographers who made that spirit known to us.

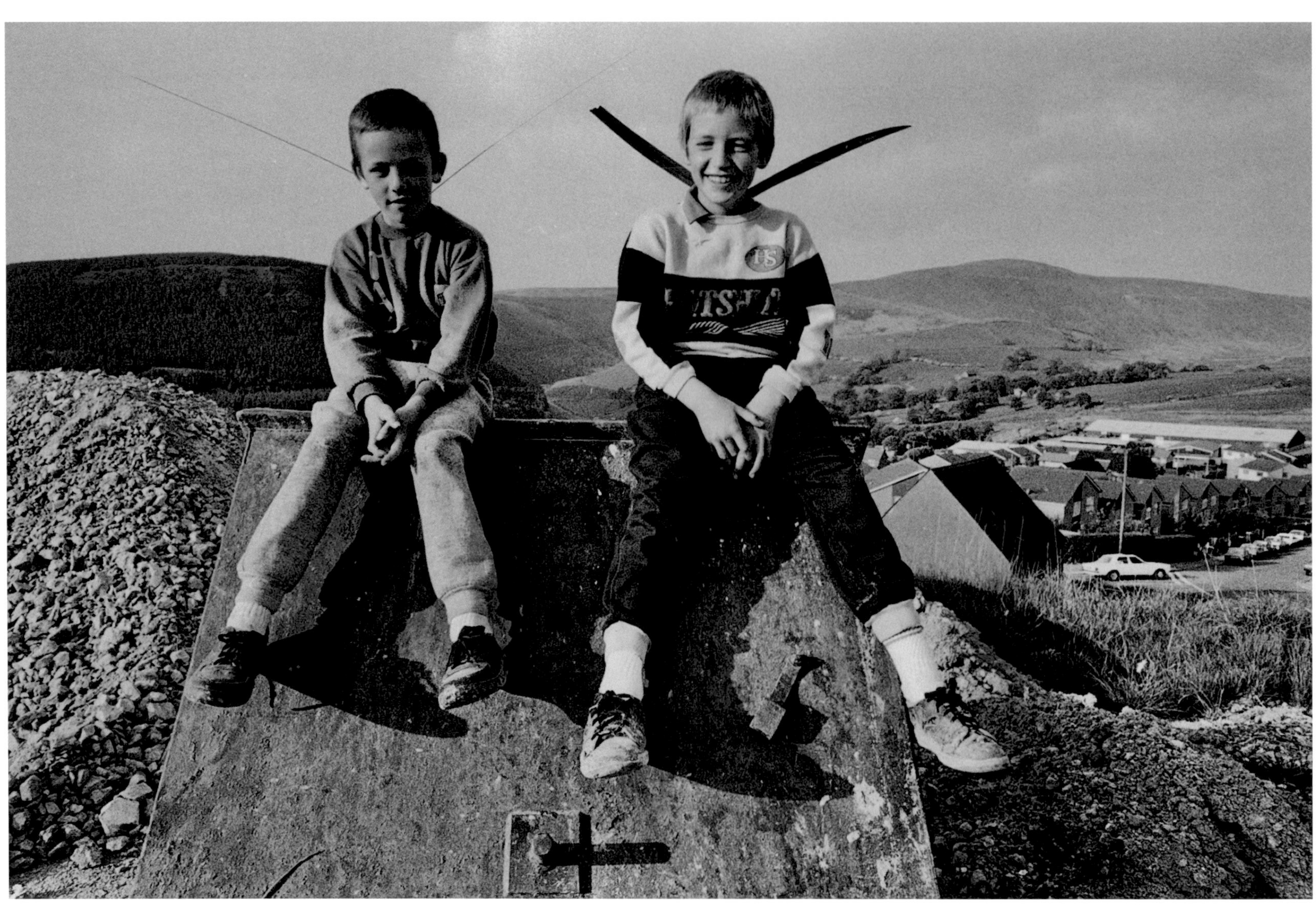

Cul-de-Sac

Through A Lens Darkly

Osi Rhys Osmond

This book comes to us as readers and viewers with a strange duality. It comes to challenge and it comes to praise. It comes to challenge those that have power over other people's lives, and to passionately accuse those who dispense that power in such a cavalier fashion. It is, in that sense, an indictment. And it comes, primarily perhaps, to praise those, the subjects of these photographs, who by their persistence, optimism and social energy have constructed a meaningful culture out of tragic and traumatic circumstances. And it is, in that sense, an acclamation. Additionally these images, words and recordings exist to confront those deeply embedded stereotypes of representation that the mining community have traditionally suffered, and to offer documentation as an act of social witness that records and gives voice to a people who usually remain unheard.

I cannot look at these photographs, the text or the accompanying DVD, without feeling an enormous sense of anger and shame. These people are my people and this community is similar to the community from which I come, and in which many of my family still live. What has happened to these people? What has happened to this place? Why have they, their community and communities like theirs across South Wales been abandoned to face the ravages of post-industrialisation with less consideration for their needs than that given to the natural world that surrounds them? The answer seems to be that the physical environment of the South Wales Valleys is now a commodity that can be traded in the tourist markets of the world. The people and mining culture that created this landscape cannot be commodified, other than as caricatures or museum attendants, so sadly they are no longer necessary. They have become a people stranded by history as the great wealth of the coalfield bypassed the communities that produced it leaving them with deep social and physical scars, powerful collective memories and an extraordinary and very necessary social resilience in the face of the constructive indifference of the political elites.

The coalfields of Britain, particularly the mining valleys of South Wales, have been a site of struggle and contention since the rapid acceleration of deep mining at the beginning of the 19th century. The establishment powers quickly saw those communities as a potent threat to political and social order as hordes of migrant workers from Wales and beyond poured in to create a novel and unfamiliar society. From their beginnings and especially during the mid 19th century struggle for social justice and political rights they were seen as dangerous, a breeding ground for radicalism and dissent, promoting fears that the mining masses were developing into a savage beast that might well prove impossible to control. With the demise of deep mining and the ensuing endemic unemployment, the policy of treating the economically bereft as problematic and socially contagious continues and is clearly evident in the isolation of these communities, not just naturally by geography, but politically as the governing hegemony ignores their dire circumstances, while taking their political allegiance for granted.

One of the chief problems of depicting the mining and post mining communities is that both the people and the places have made and continue to make very compelling images. The compositional dynamic of the familiar pit-head winding gear and the characteristic faces of the people, miners or their families, have offered a very potent subject matter for artists, photographers and film makers. Now, the aesthetic certainties of the past are being overtaken and undermined by new ways of seeing and the post- industrial world needs a new grammar of representation. The traditional pictorial representation of mining communities is well understood in both painting and photography. Depictions have often been loaded with a peculiar and constantly changing mix of fear, sentimentality and cautious romanticism. The newspapers of the early 19th century saw the novel mining settlements as newsworthy, a convenient source of images that engendered social unease among the new middle class city dweller. They were good for sales though, as the press barons of Victorian Britain placed our mining communities in the same category as contemporary 'redtops' put the illegal immigrant or asylum seeker of today: as the unpredictable and dangerous other. And interestingly, although their political radicalism threatened bourgeois society, mining disasters made compelling stories, having all the necessary narrative ingredients of waiting and tension, suffering, loss and episodic unfolding that made the next edition eagerly anticipated, a melodramatic approach that remains the standard media response.

The limitations of Victorian printing processes meant that newspaper images were published in black and white, by means of engravings made from drawings initially and later from photographs. The medium of engraving profoundly influenced the construction of a formal language of representation for the mining communities, soon reinforced and confirmed by the arrival of photography. The early cameras affected ensuing depictions, as the slow shutter was unable to express action, which continued to be the province of the engraving, and subjects had to be carefully posed, with the result that they tended to portray the miner and even the community as a type, clearly seen in the work of William Clayton in the mid 1800s. This view persisted into the 20th century and developed into an anthropological representation of the mining classes as an exotic other to be pictured in a grittily romantic manner. A later exception to this, at the beginning of the 20th century, was W. E. Jones, who, coming from that community, made much more celebratory photographs of the mining world than those

which preceded him and many that were to follow. By the depressions of the twenties and thirties photographs of mining communities, especially those of South Wales, naturally reflected the much gloomier public mood. Bill Brandt and Edith Tudor Hart, who visited South Wales in the 1930s, heralded in some respects the later photographic work of the American, Walker Evans, who, while commissioned under the Rural Resettlement Administration, created a powerful aesthetic of economic deprivation that rapidly became the norm for representations of depression period social degradation. Edith Tudor Hart's work demonstrates great human sympathy, gracefully depicting children and the domestic among the industrial, and while much of Brandt's work showing the miners in their workplace focused strongly on abstract values, his images of the miner at home, eating, resting or washing, often with the aid of his wife, are gentle and compassionate.

The very nature of the coal industry, with its ubiquitous black spoil, created an atmosphere that easily lent itself to the grainy exigencies of the black and white photography of the time. Carefully composed representations of this dusty world seemed naturally ordained to appear in a darkly carboniferous pictorial conspiracy as a form of visual political confirmation. It can be argued that for much of the mid 20th century these 'types' were almost always shown as the heroic scapegoat, the convenient sacrificial victim, who would suffer with dignity, for all our sins on the altar of capitalist excess and exploitation. Although it is possible to suggest that the mining community was itself compliant in the con-

struction of certain ongoing stereotypes, some practitioners, chiefly photo-journalists, encouraged suitably melodramatic poses and it is evident that as soon as a formal language of representation had come into being, the subjects themselves quickly learned what was expected of them as they faced the camera.

And so they did, in the work of a wide range of practitioners: from Brandt and Tudor Hart and later Eugene Smith in the forties and Robert Frank in the fifties. Films including *Proud Valley*, *The Citadel*, and *How Green Was My Valley* consolidated and perpetuated a formal aesthetic of romantic representation for colliery and community life. The language of representation was consolidated and confirmed by the work of artists, many of who were from the mining community, some, like Vincent Evans and Archie Rhys Griffiths, even having been colliery workers themselves. These examinations of working class society were continued more critically in the documentary film movement that began in the thirties and from which the Mass Observation project developed: begun by Humphrey Jennings and others in the 1930s and focusing strongly on the mining industry. Jennings himself went on to make *Silent Village* during the Second World War, a film in which the Welsh mining village of Cwmgiedd stood in for a defiant Czech community ravaged by savage revenge during Nazi German occupation. Jill Craigie's 1949 film *Blue Scar* carried on the tradition of mining documentaries, this time celebrating the recent nationalisation of the industry that became the National Coal Board and rapidly established its own documentary film unit.

As well as documentaries, feature films such as *The Citadel* and *How Green Was My Valley* demonstrated an admiration of and sympathy for the mining community. These films reflected appreciation of the strong and timely anti-fascist sentiments and brotherly solidarity that underwrote the international socialism of the miner's major political ideologies; for many, they and their communities were a living embodiment of the socialist dream.

In 1966 the Aberfan disaster saw many pitiful images in the press and television of a mining community in trauma. Later the American photographer I. C. Rapoport spent time living with the bereaved community and photographed the slow process of a society regaining its collective composure in a series of touching, dramatic and melancholy black and white images. By now the end of the South Wales coal industry was in sight and the remaining mining communities were haunted by the threat of closure and redundancy.

Shortly after Aberfan, and deeply affected, Karl Francis, himself from a mining family, began his career as a film maker, writing and directing a number of moving, naturalistic, drama-documentary films, including *Above Us the Earth* that extolled the resistance and radicalism of mining communities under threat of colliery closure. Since then, David Hurn and Philip Jones Griffiths and Ffotogallery's *Valley Project* have photographed the collapse, death throes and post mortem of a declining industry and its damaged society in black and white images that discreetly confirmed, smiled at and demolished some of the longstanding representational clichés. Roger Tiley, a photographer from the mining community, photographs the post mining valleys using a traditional documentary approach to working class life, extending his interest into an international concern for heavy industry and its workers. Recently, younger photographers like Paul Cabutts have looked in a completely new way at the mining valleys, giving an ironic post-modern twist to long-standing pictorial expectations. Overall, the mining community is probably the most photographed industrial subject of photographic history.

This powerful and perceptive publication, coming as it does some time after the demise of deep mining in the upper Afan Valley, shows the community and landscape twenty or more years after the closure of the local collieries. The photographs and filmed interviews were made more than fifteen years ago, but very little has changed since then. The people and their enclosing valley are sympathetically depicted as stranded in a geographic cul-de-sac where industrial history itself has come to a dead end. Today in these communities it seems as though history has passed by, they are in a strange sense stranded, standing outside history.

Although the last mine in the upper Afan Valley had closed as early as 1969, large numbers of local men continued to travel to the mines of the adjacent valleys and this remained a mining community long after the local mines had gone. Following the sudden tragedy of initial closure, the gradual death of adjacent collieries and associated job losses initiated a slow haemorrhage of optimism. The rhythm of such events, unrelenting and unavoidable, can shock a community in the manner of a gradually unfolding natural disaster. The trauma, though not immediately perceptible, is, however, as profound as that triggered by a major earthquake or tornado.

To visit the upper Afan Valley now is to enter a time warp, a place where two unconnected histories seem to be unfolding. Two different realities confront the visitor, on the one hand the very evident reality of unrelenting post-industrial change and neglect, and on the other the brave new official optimism of rebranding, where the leaflet reigns supreme, shiny and hyperbolic, promising a rebirth for this community and a fabulous future for the valley as the hub of a carefully planned tourist industry that will create the employment opportunities of future generations.

As we have seen, in the wake of post-industrial decline each individual feels redundant, and eventually so does the whole community. In these isolated valleys the promise of new work has yet to materialise to any meaningful extent. To make the area attractive to visitors, large amounts of public funding have been committed to remedial landscape work, efforts that have been largely cosmetic, acting as a kind of post-industrial botox. The smile has disappeared from the landscape and is replaced by the rictus grin of the unnaturally realigned. The Glyncorrwg Ponds project, welcomed and eagerly accepted as almost a local idea at its inception, has become to some bitter evidence of the failure of such schemes, although it functions perfectly well as a fishing facility. Among the filmed interviews the disappointed expectant workforce of unemployed local men air their views and they do so in a very trenchant manner. The many visitors to the extremely popular cycle trails come for an adventure that utilises the wild landscape in a promiscuously short-term relationship with the geography that bypasses the social reality of life after coal for the local population. That outsiders enjoy their breathless leisure time in full view of a society in decline makes a harrowing accompaniment to the deeply felt hopelessness of the long-term unemployed. The interviews encompass every generation, from veteran colliery workers and former railway employees to young men, young mothers and their children. Their words reveal the reality of life 'after coal' for many of those left behind in the aftermath of industrial decline.

Nevertheless, considering the fate that has befallen their community the people of the Upper Afan Valley remain friendly and unexpectedly optimistic. The pubs and shops, although many fewer than in the old days, are still very welcoming, as are the homes, for the people are as hospitable as they have always been. The betting office was among the warmest and most inviting places in Croeserw. Carpeted and snug and with a regular clientele discussing form while large wall-to-wall television monitors were simultaneously showing all the events on which it is possible to place a bet, mostly horse races, beamed by satellite from one glitteringly successful social milieu into a very different reality. The physical wellbeing of the horses, never mind their owners, their energetic beauty, shiny flanks and highly toned limbs contrast strangely with the pallor of many of the gamblers.

Looking at the images in this series I am constantly reminded of the time I spent in Palestine. There, another community with even greater social, political and employment problems, and the sense of powerlessness that they engender, constantly awaits unfolding events with trepidation. The people in these photographs stare out at the lens and appear in one sense to outstare it. There is the feeling of transience, languor, of time moving slowly, of discontinuity or hiatus as a condition of life. Expectant waiting is the sole continuance; people are out in the world, watchful, looking at a world passing them by. Those photographed are an inseparable part of the landscape, and in the strange way that the topography of the valleys tilts our visual perspective, their presence against the rising background, whether inside their homes and social spaces or out in the landscape, emphasises their deep attachment to the very earth, houses and architecture of their villages and environs.

Strangely, the recent past, when re-examined through the photograph, can sometimes look more remote than the distant past. The earlier black and white images spoke effectively to previous times, although these post-coal pictures, having shed the dull sheen of the black dust, confirm the final eclipse of coal, now merely a memory. The ubiquitous dust darkly flavoured the whole atmosphere of the mining world; now the new clarity in the air is best served by images in colour. This is a physical phenomenon rather than a social one, and some might observe that the bright photographic hues reflect the fact that we live in more chemically enhanced times and that this more accurately mirrors the harsh social realities of the present. The conflict between the beauty in the image making and the hardships of those depicted creates a pictorial tension, a visual dilemma as photography as a political act and photography as interrogation becomes hostage to photography as an artistic quest. That, in this case, is done knowingly, for in their engagement with the people the photographers have successfully resolved questions of responsibility and complicity, power and exploitation to the satisfaction of both parties.

For although made so many years ago, these thoughtful, beautiful and powerfully constructed, coloured images convey a fascinating pictorial intrigue and a very contemporary vitality that is a reflection of the willing and enthusiastic co-operation of all the participants. And it is this that makes this work so distinctive; from its inception, the artists, Tina Carr and Annemarie Schöne have been committed to a collaborative project that immediately and properly involved the community in its creative philosophy. The people depicted are not simply the subject of the photographs, they inhabit them and contribute to them, are a very real part of them and of the process of bringing them into being. Therefore, these revealing photographs are not condescending in the way that many of the earlier ones were, largely because the characters depicted are able to positively influence the terms of their own representation. Many of the earlier images told us only about the superficial appearance of the subjects and from this we can have very little idea of the actuality of the lives depicted, as they are usually seen not as lives but as ciphers for a particular social or political viewpoint, used to illustrate something other than the reality of the subjects' own experience. In these photographs we are closer to seeing people as they see themselves and that is the essential difference between these tenderly revealing photographs and the earlier and more deliberately aesthetically bleak documentary images. Throughout the exercise the artists have been at pains to highlight the positive attributes of the community, the keen gardeners, the mechanics, home-makers, people with social skills, hobbies and many other attributes that are often overlooked by officialdom. There was the hope that this project could become a kind of audit, a way of enabling the community to realise hope beyond their present difficulties. The newer interventions, like the Communities First scheme, have taken these ideas as their starting point, but critically, until people feel a sense of ownership their beneficial engagement will never be fully realised.

The dramatic appearance of the physical landscapes as one approaches the valleys of South Wales has softened since the demise of deep mining. Then the feeling of entering another world was palpable and the strange otherness of this place naturally drew seekers after an objectification of certain aesthetic and societal values. Those conditions, social, topographical, natural and man-made, combined with the newly arrived and diverse workforce and its dependents, resulted in a community and landscape of compelling complexity. This remains a vigourous community of extraordinary resilience; a community initially bonded together by the tribulations of harsh but interdependent mining life, although now perhaps distinguished to some degree by the injustice of abandonment. These greener gentler valleys of contemporary South Wales still carry the scars of their settlement and exploitation; a process that for the most part took place over a very short period. The historical evidence of this is clear in the landscape and in the way that events left their mark not just on the inhabitants, but on the hills, the settlements and the valley bottoms. These photographs, words and filmed interviews are important for that reason; for they hold within themselves the story of a people and a place, they have become social, physical and human archaeology. They are a record and a memorial to a changing world. They can be read and interpreted to reveal the historic story of a mining valley through the relatively short period of its birth, growth and decline as an industrial community. The intensity and rapid acceleration of change that this involved and the abrupt and traumatic catastrophe of its sudden collapse are all held within the encompassing grasp of these powerful words and images. The mines are gone, but under and above the ground this community has embedded itself in the very earth and rock into which it once tunnelled and mined, and so the people persist, they survive, they blossom and live with a defiant, cheerful natural exuberance, they construct their domestic and social stages, physically and metaphorically, they walk, they talk, box, love, marry, give birth and mourn, they play, learn, celebrate and dress up, commute, worship and garden and are photographed and so are now honoured, remembered and held fixed in time in this extraordinarily beautiful act of accusatory and celebratory documentation.

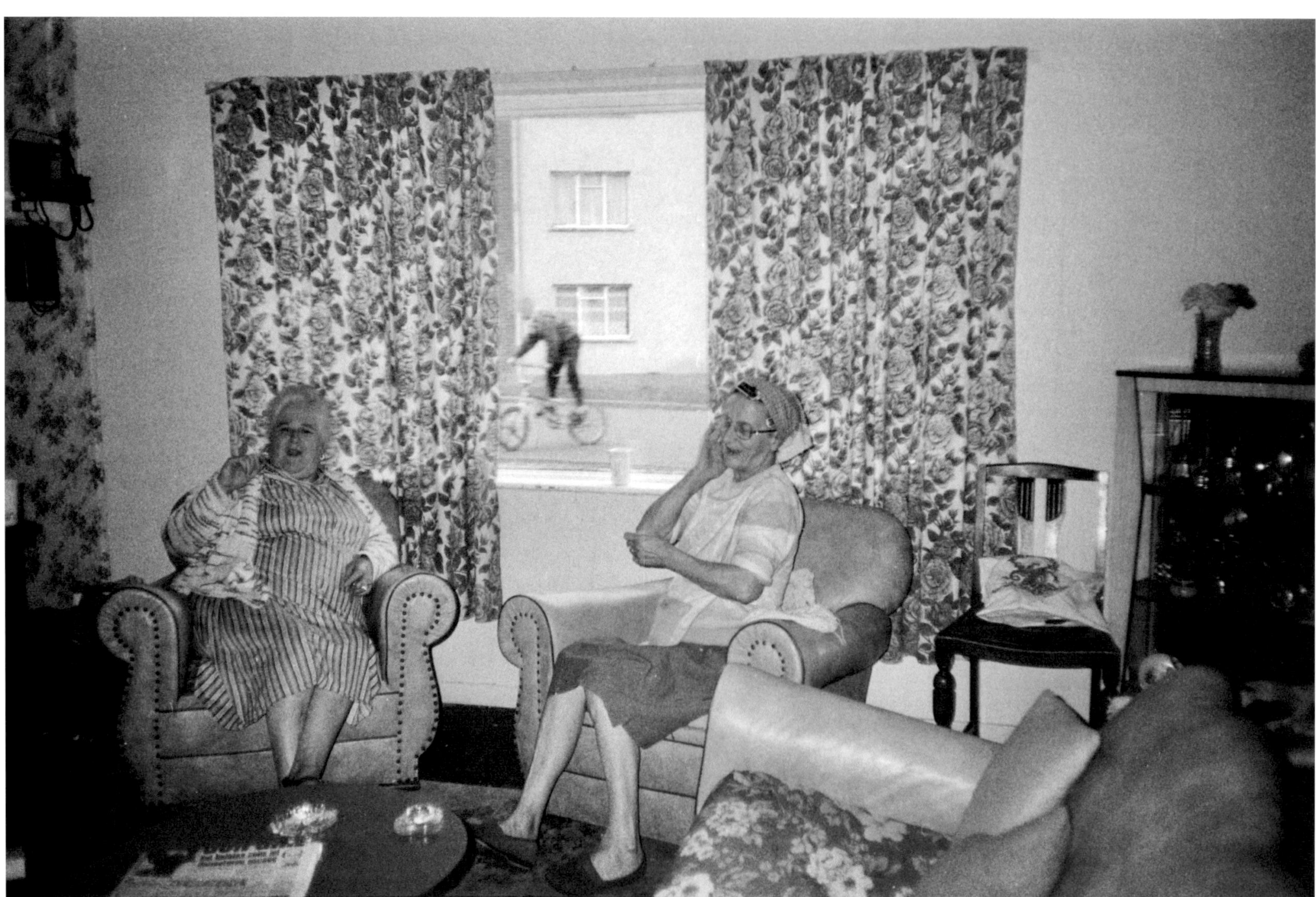

coalfaces

life after coal in the afan valley

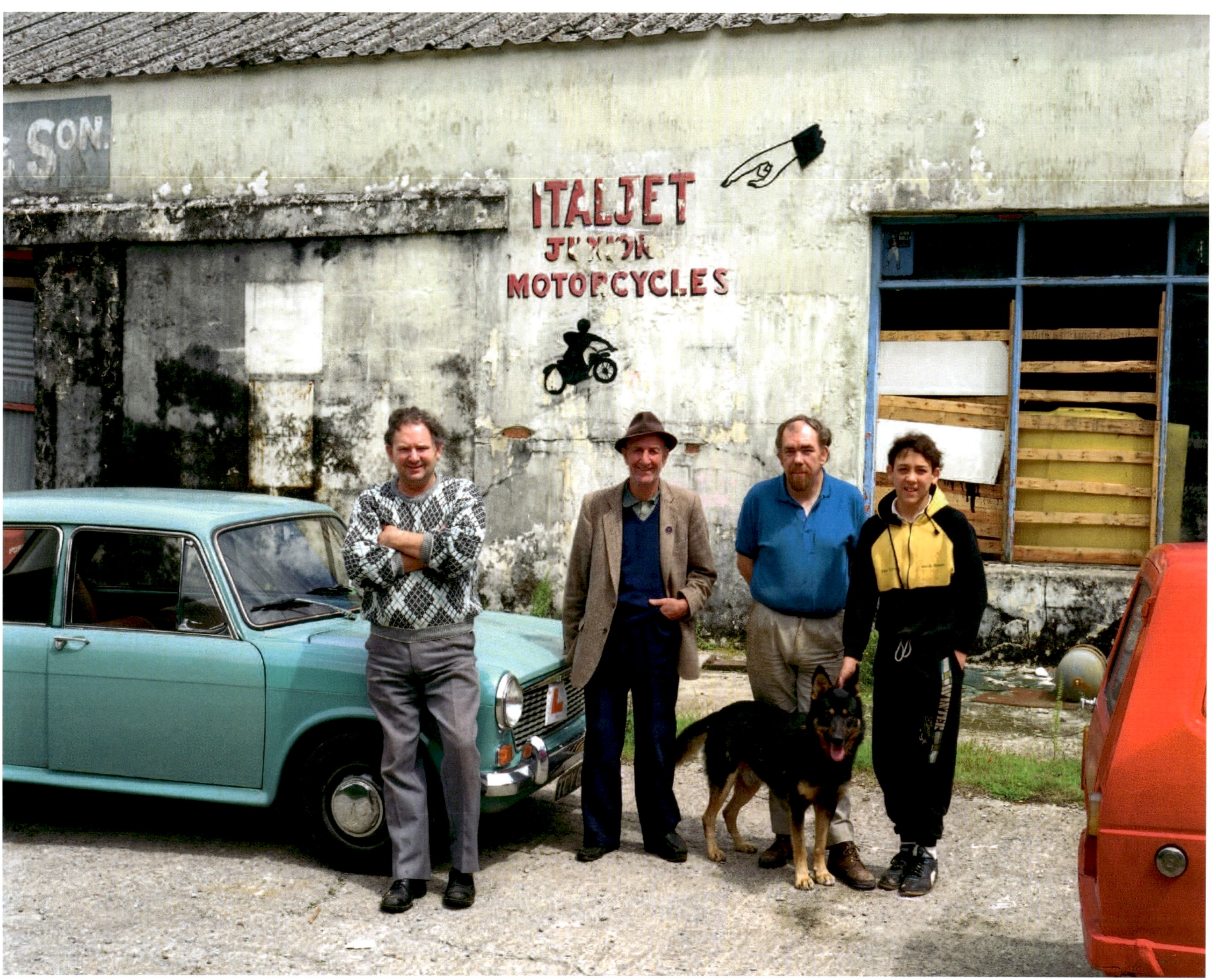

Garage, Cymmer

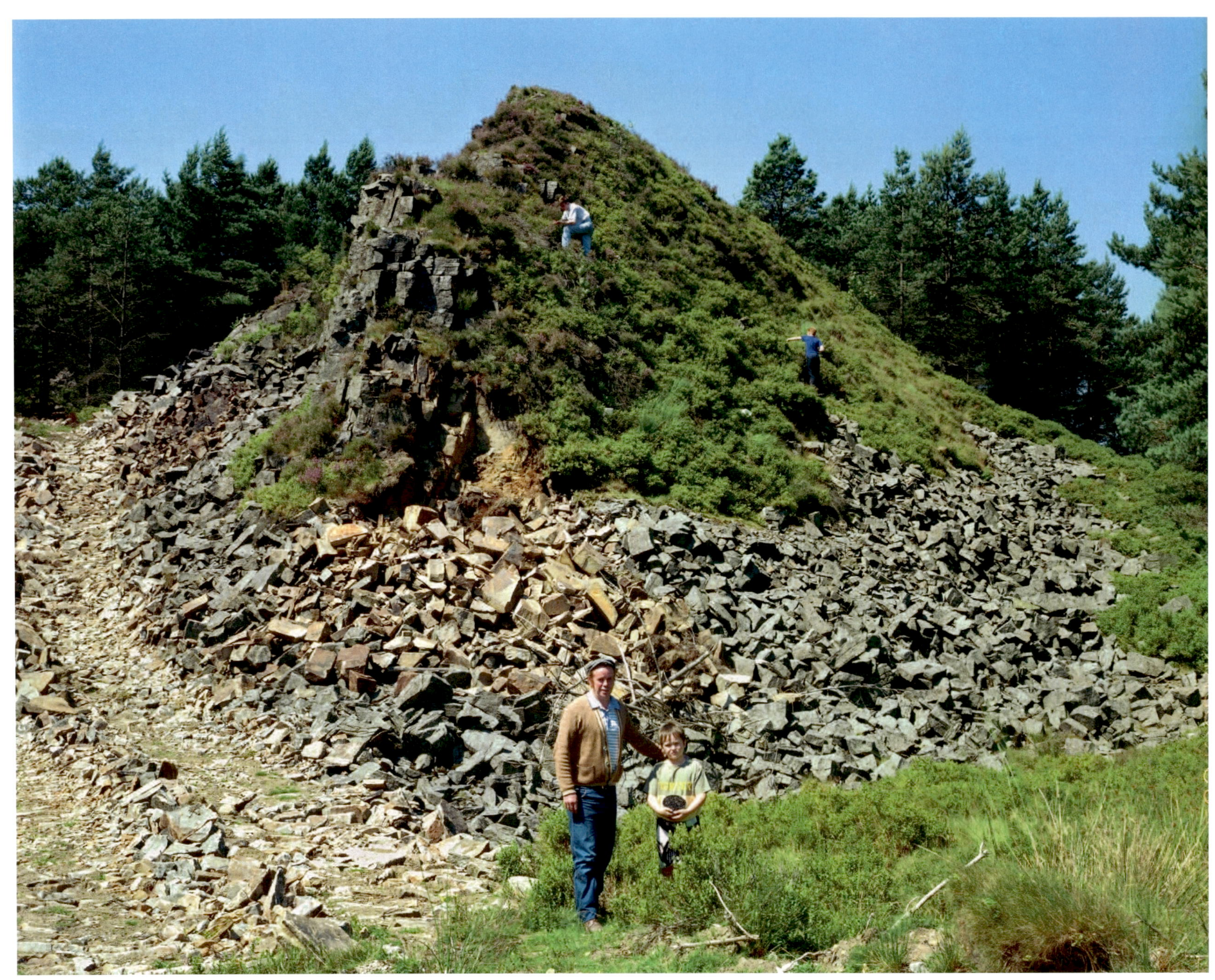

Whinberry Pickers, Caerau

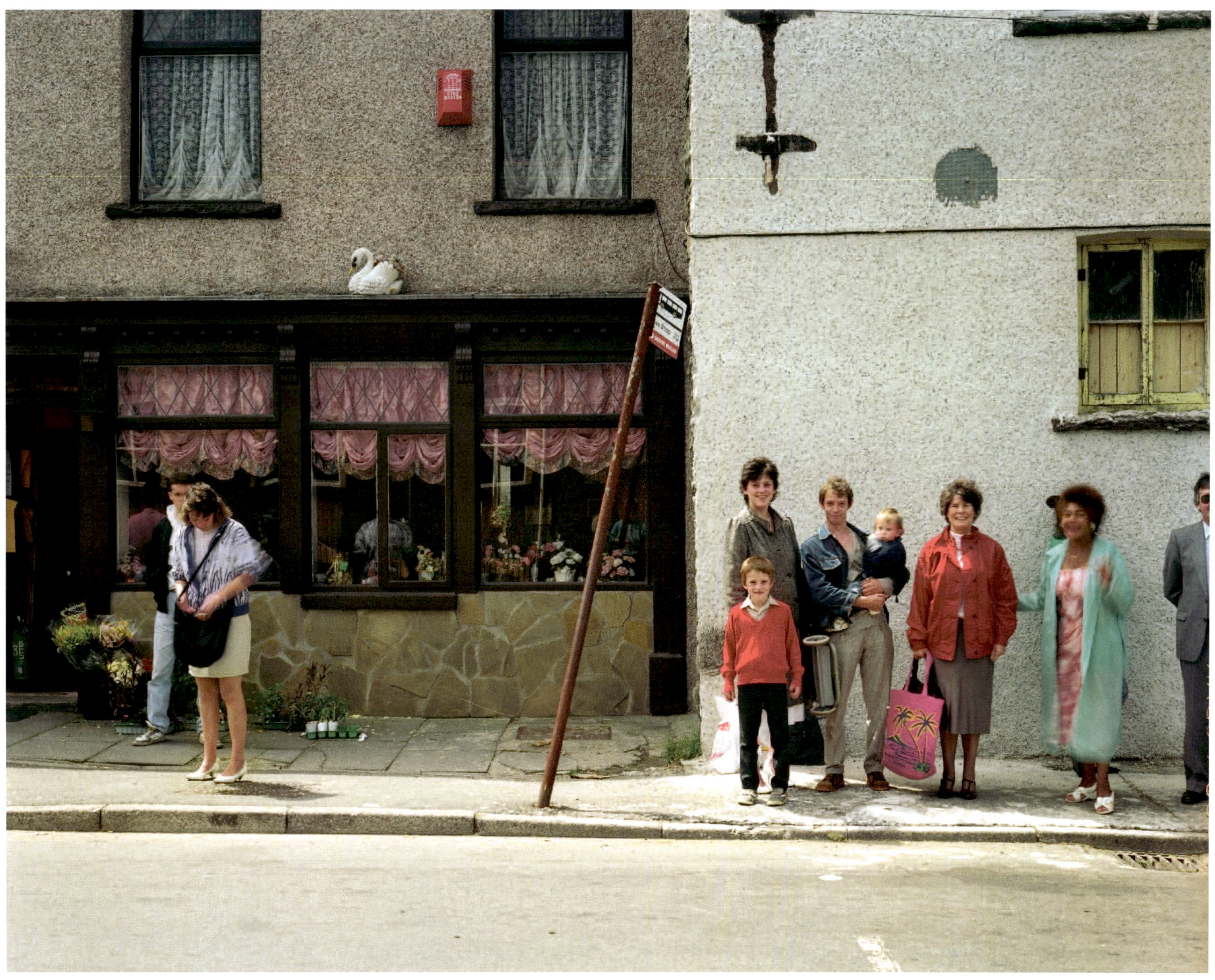

Bus Stop, Cymmer

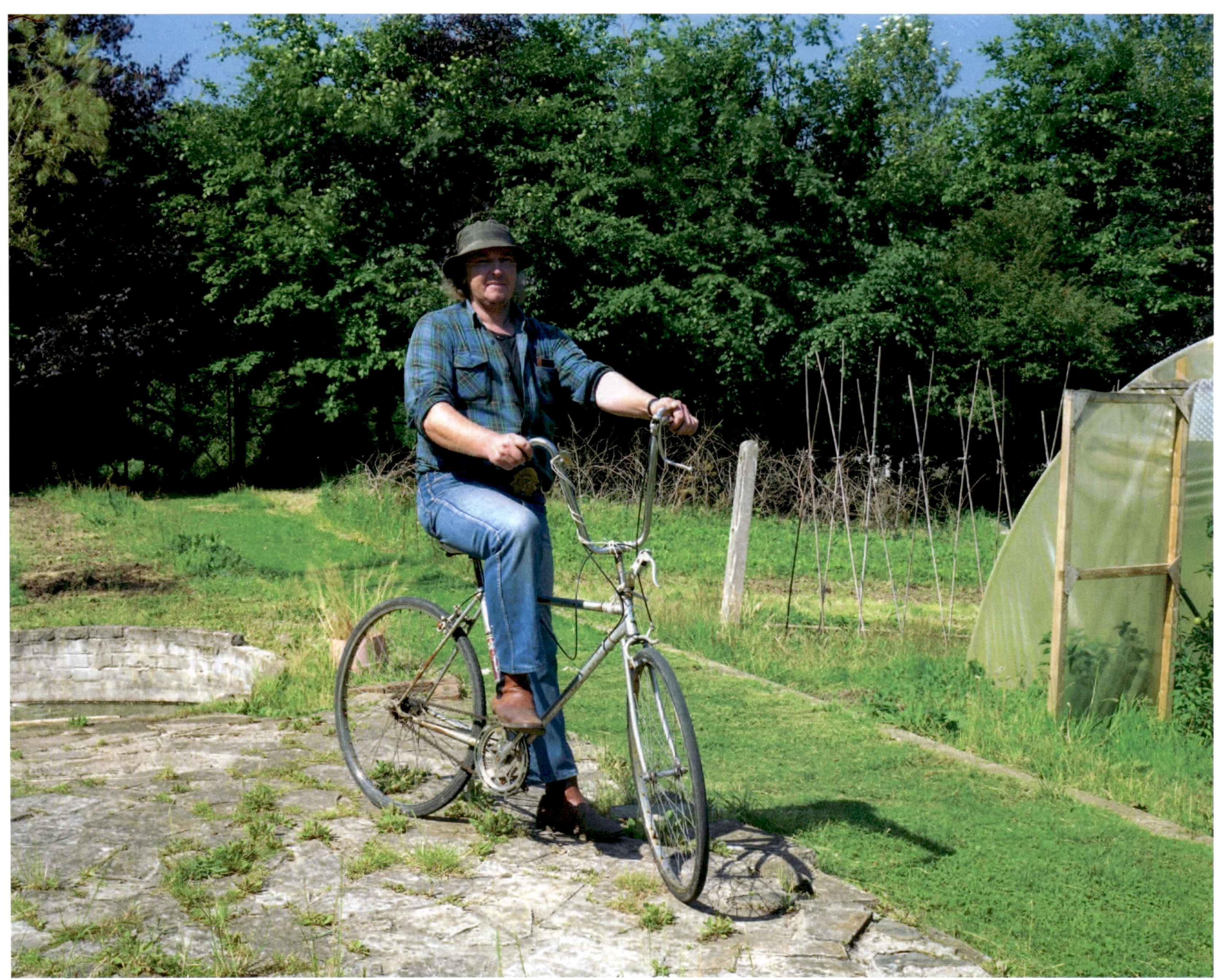

School Gardener, Cymmer

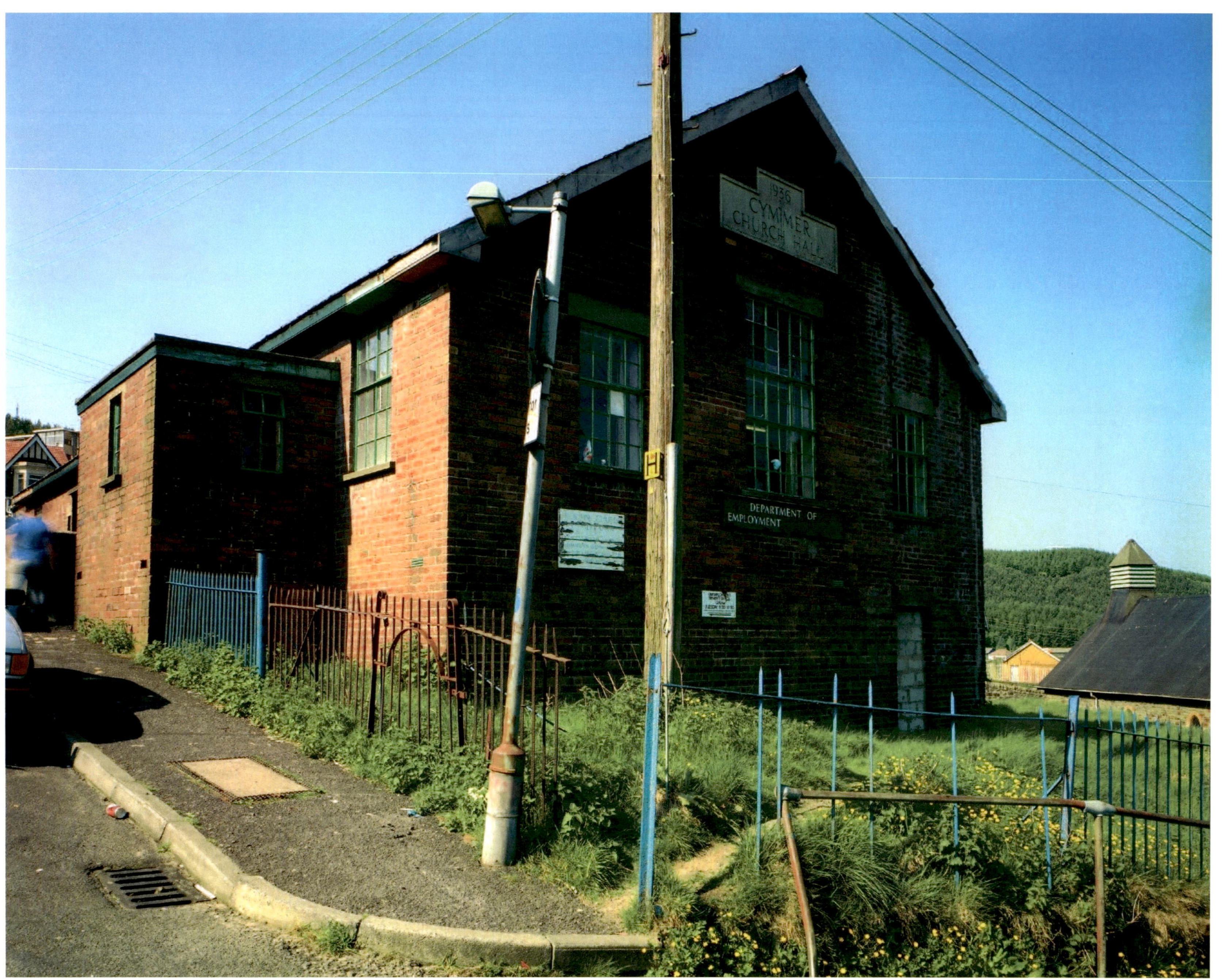

Unemployment Office, Cymmer

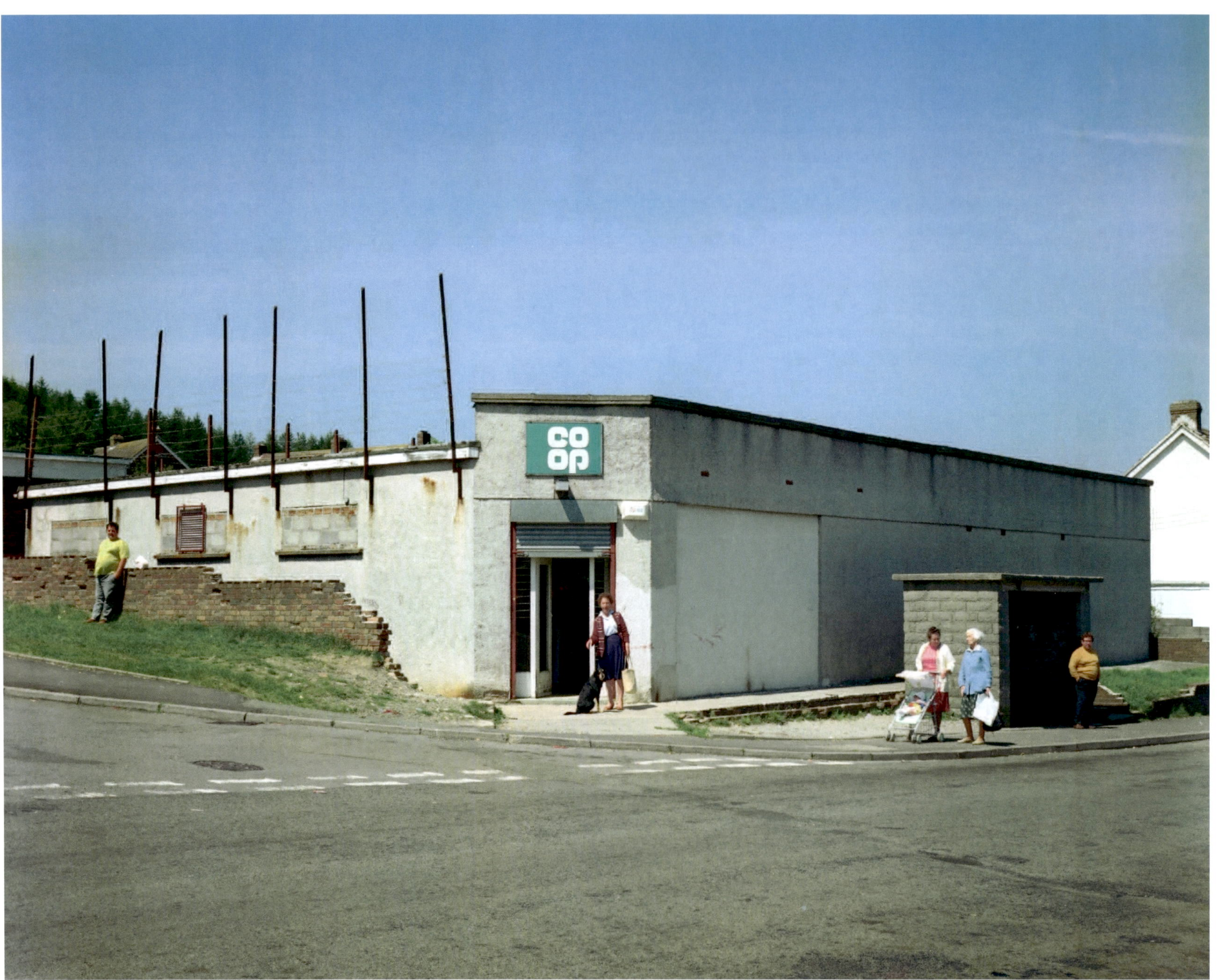

Co-op, Croeserw

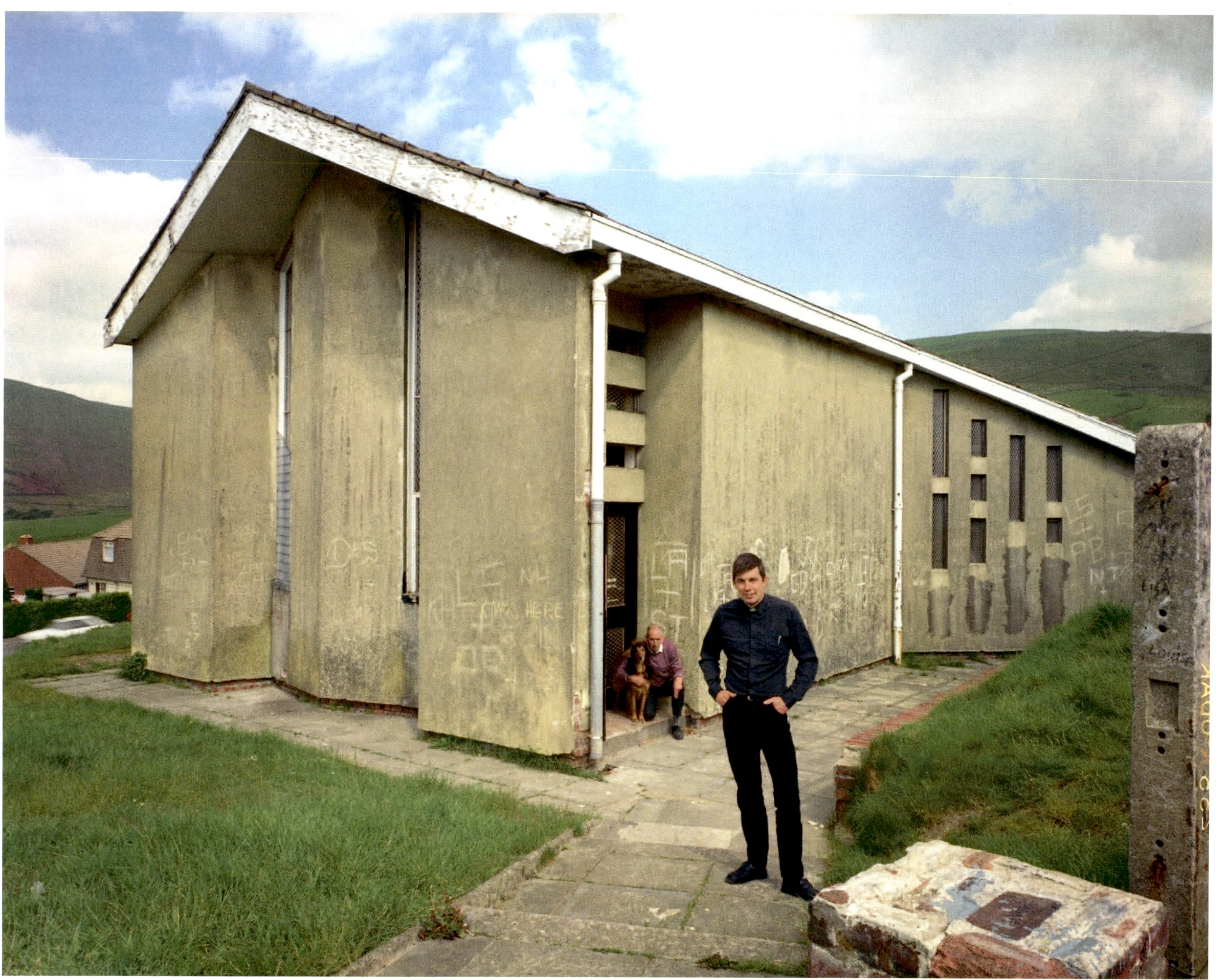

Church, Croeserw

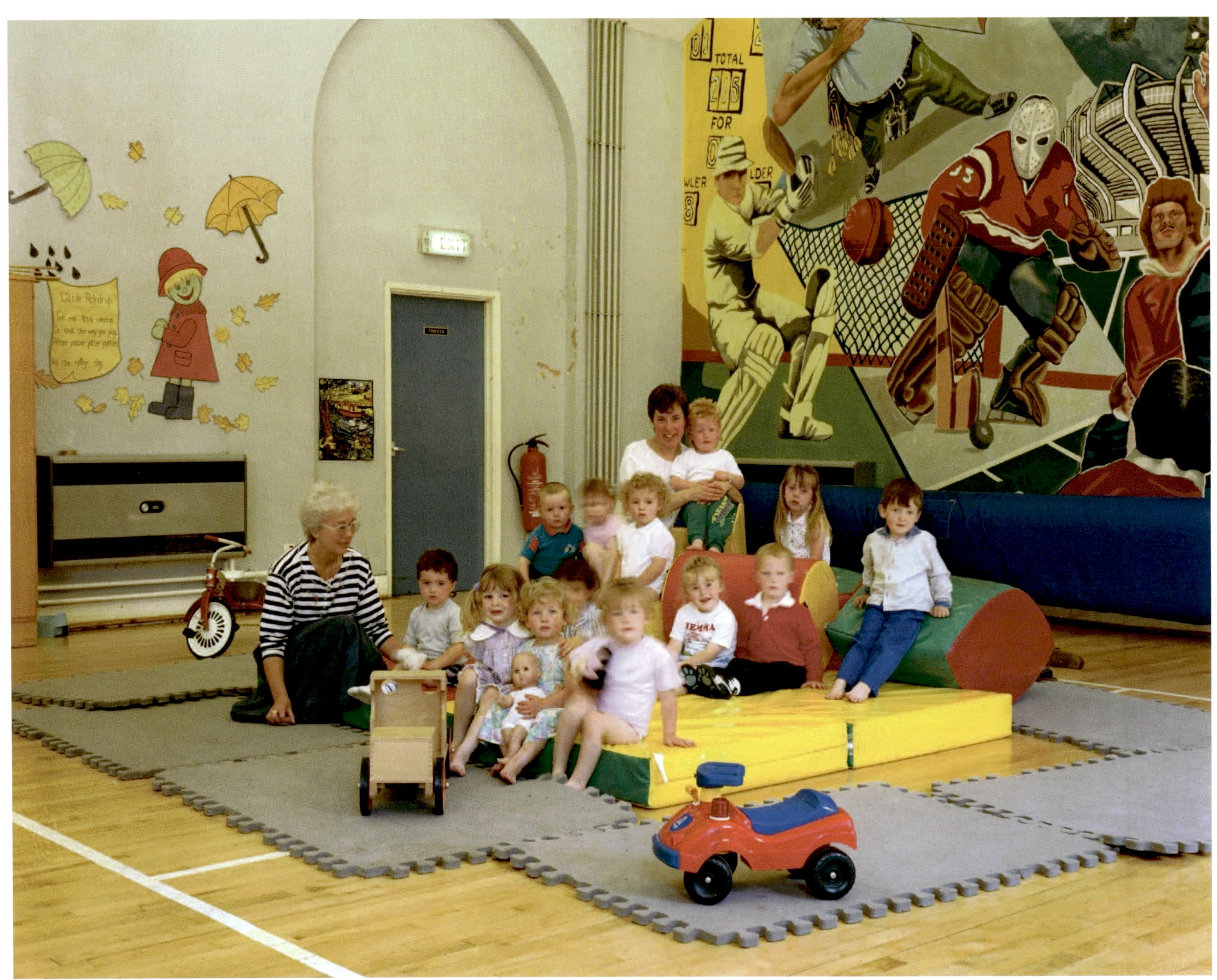

Makeshift Playgroup, CDP Hall, Cymmer

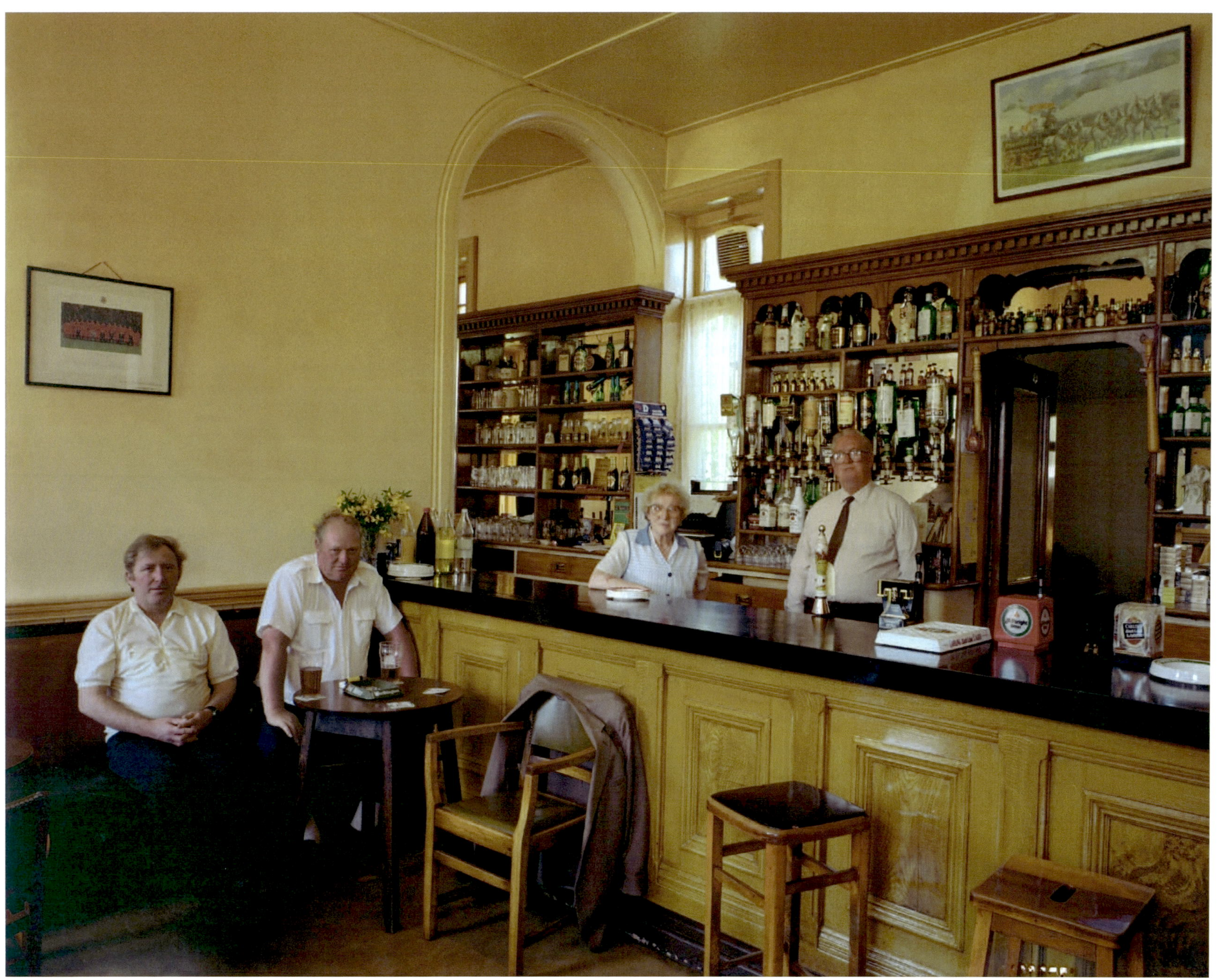

'The Refresh', Cymmer

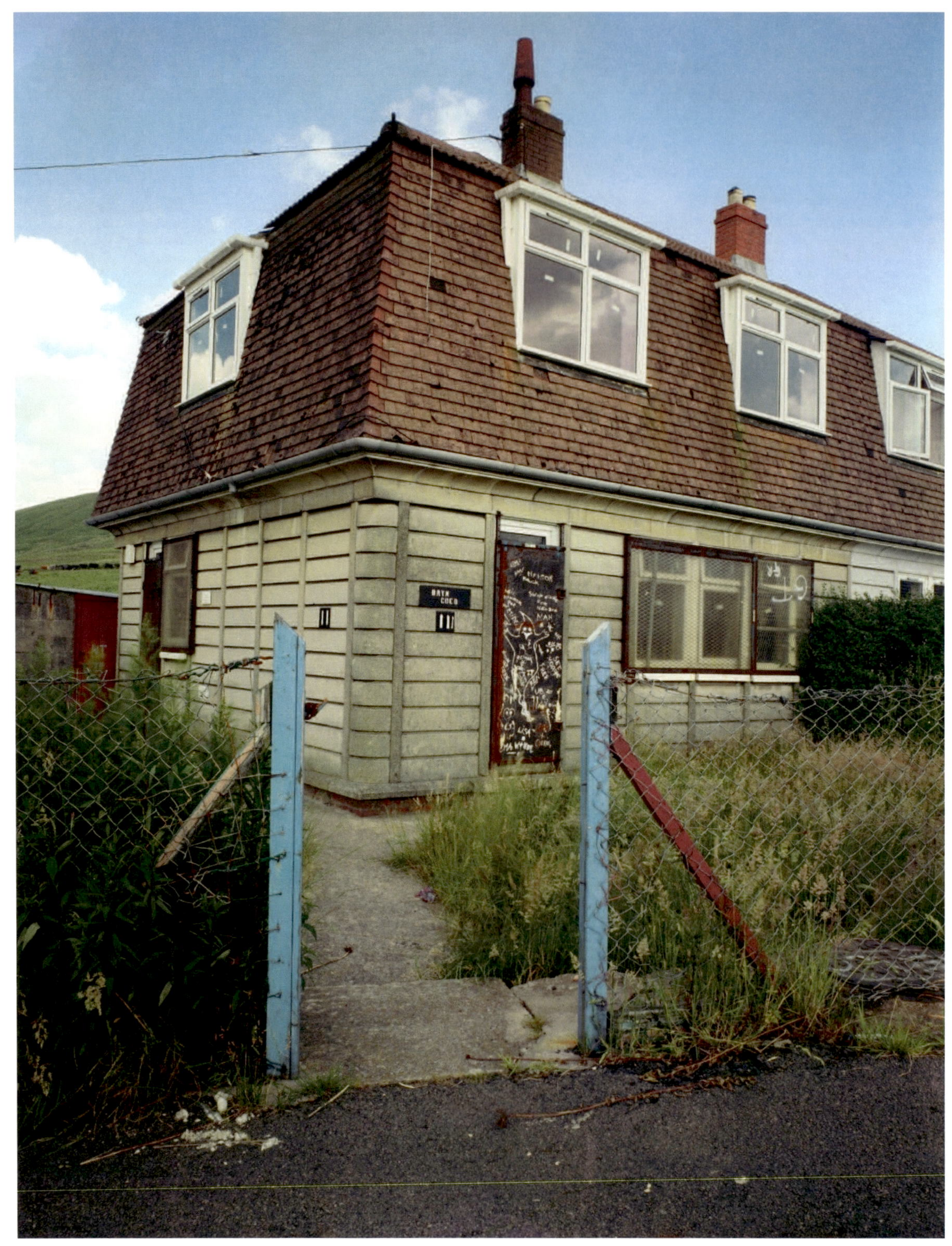

Council House, Croeserw

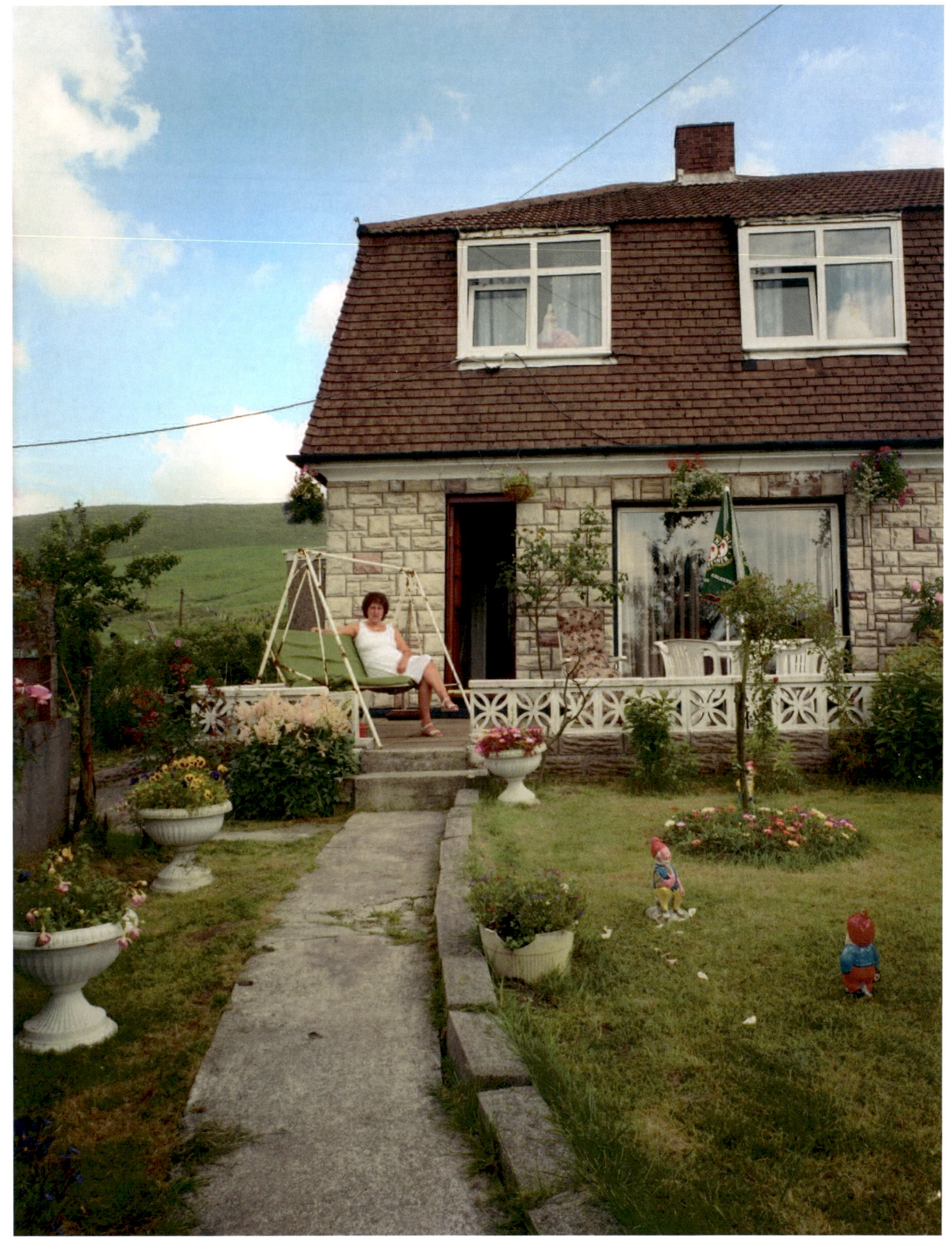

Private House, Croeserw

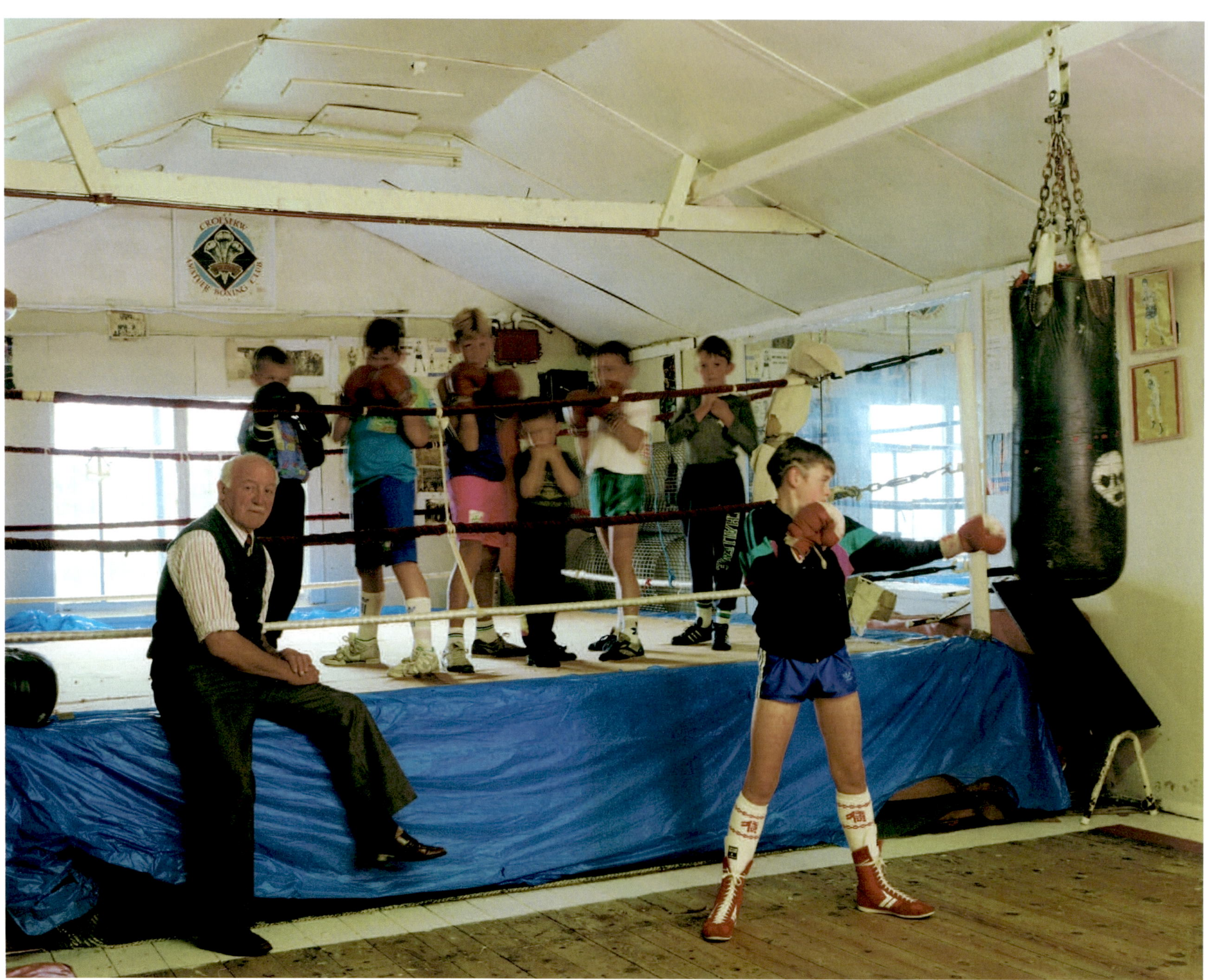

Albert and Croeserw Amateur Boxing Club

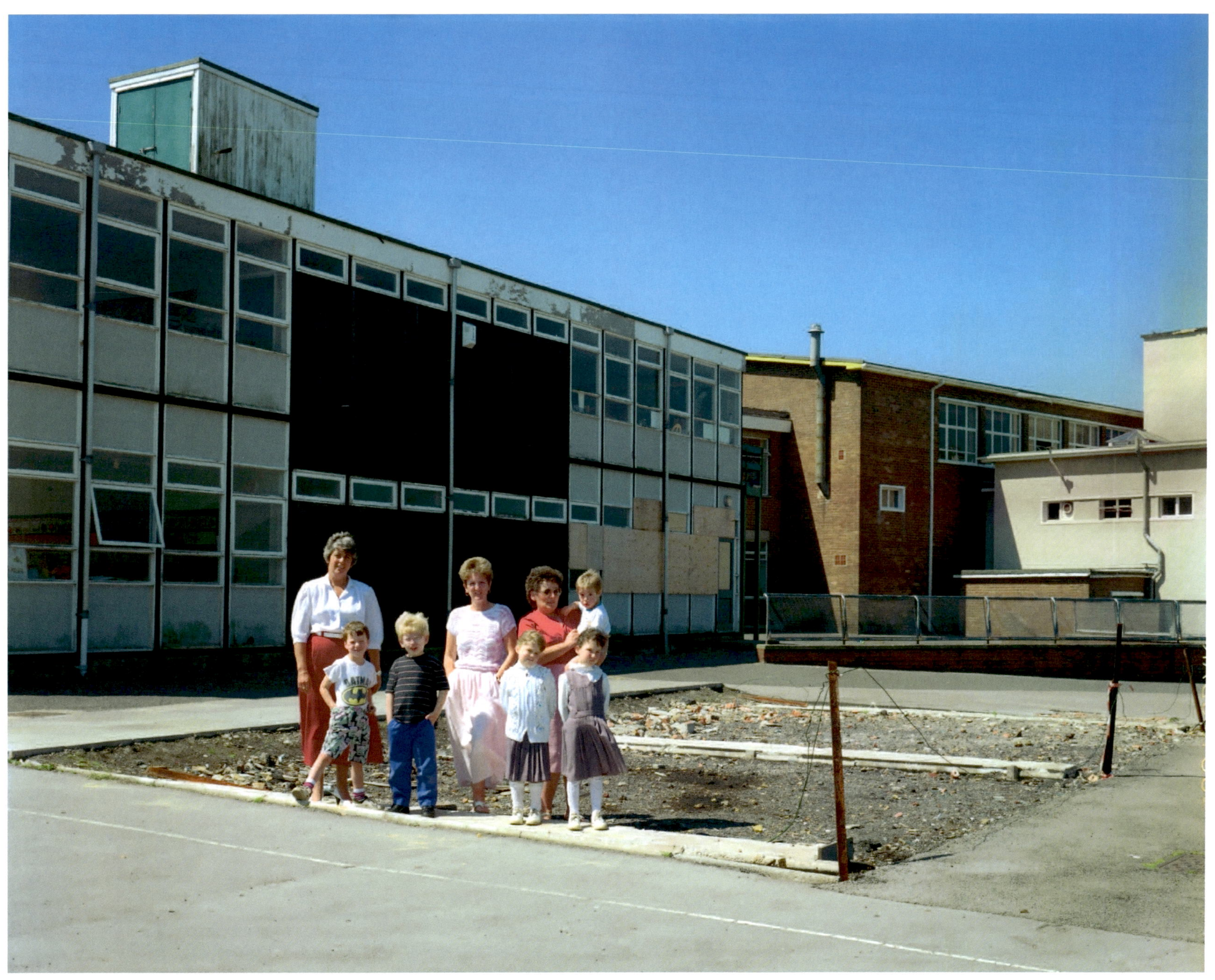

Comprehensive School, Croeserw
(Special needs unit destroyed by vandals)

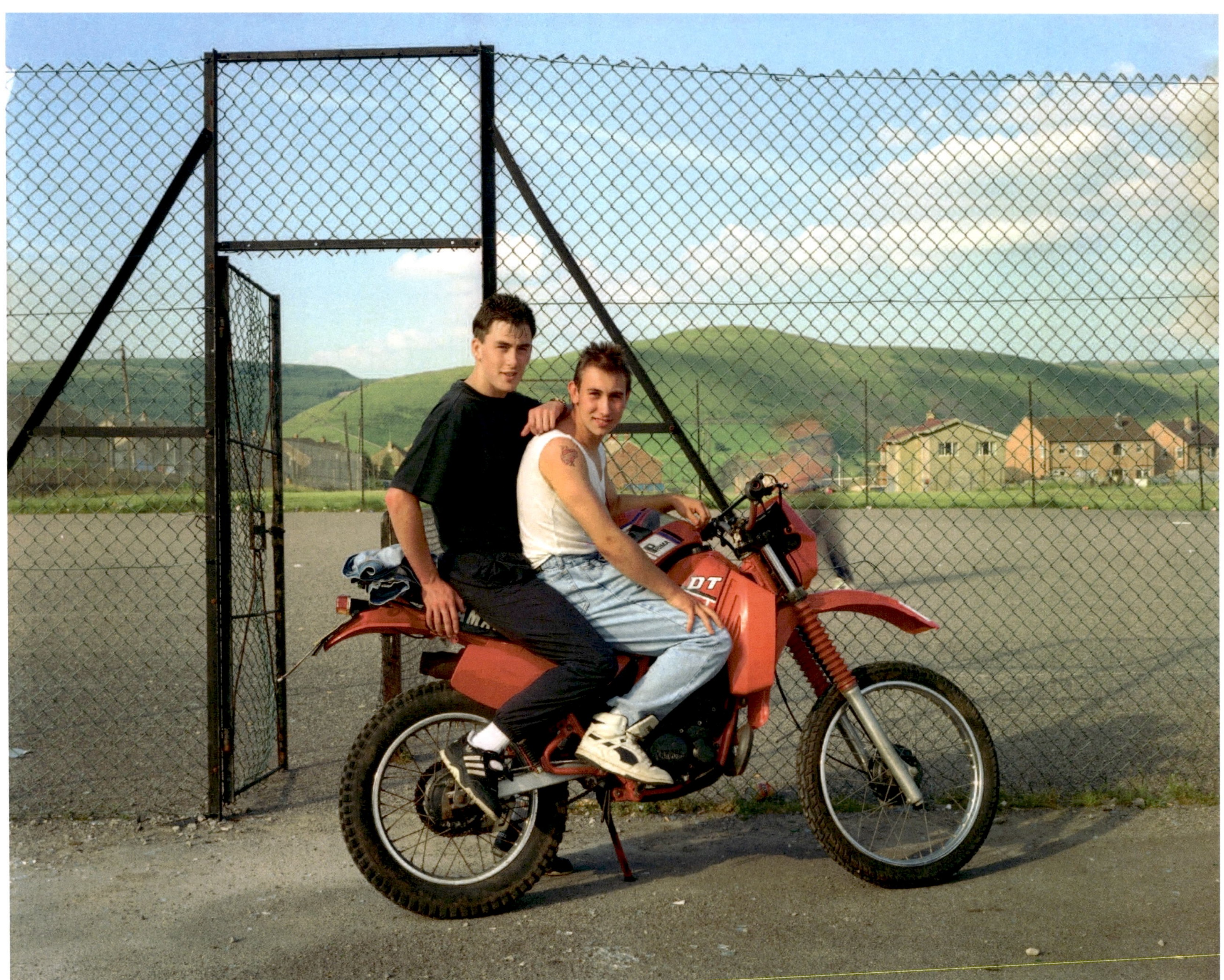

Hugh & Jason, Croeserw

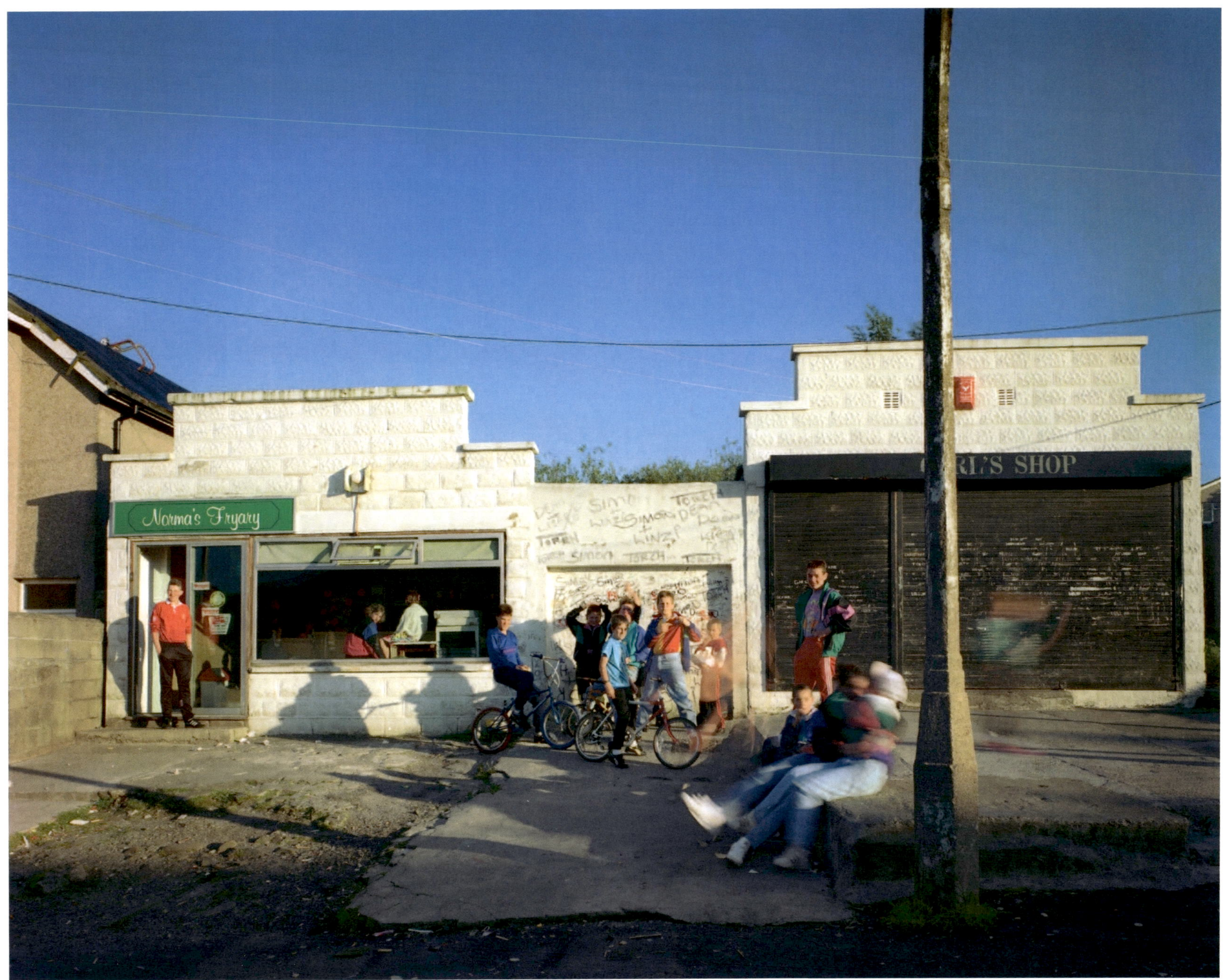

'Norma's Fryary', Croeserw

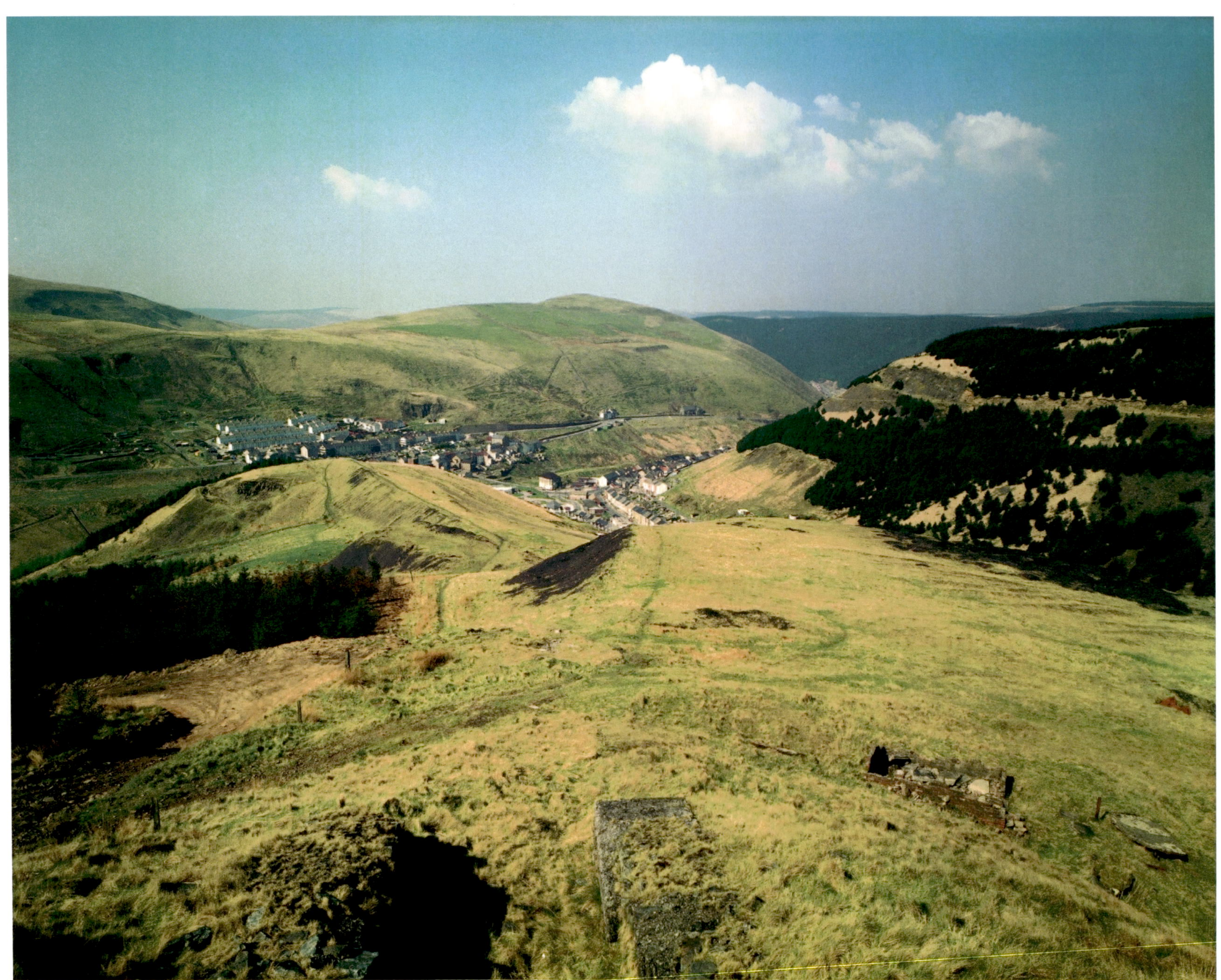

The Gwynfis from Old Mine Workings

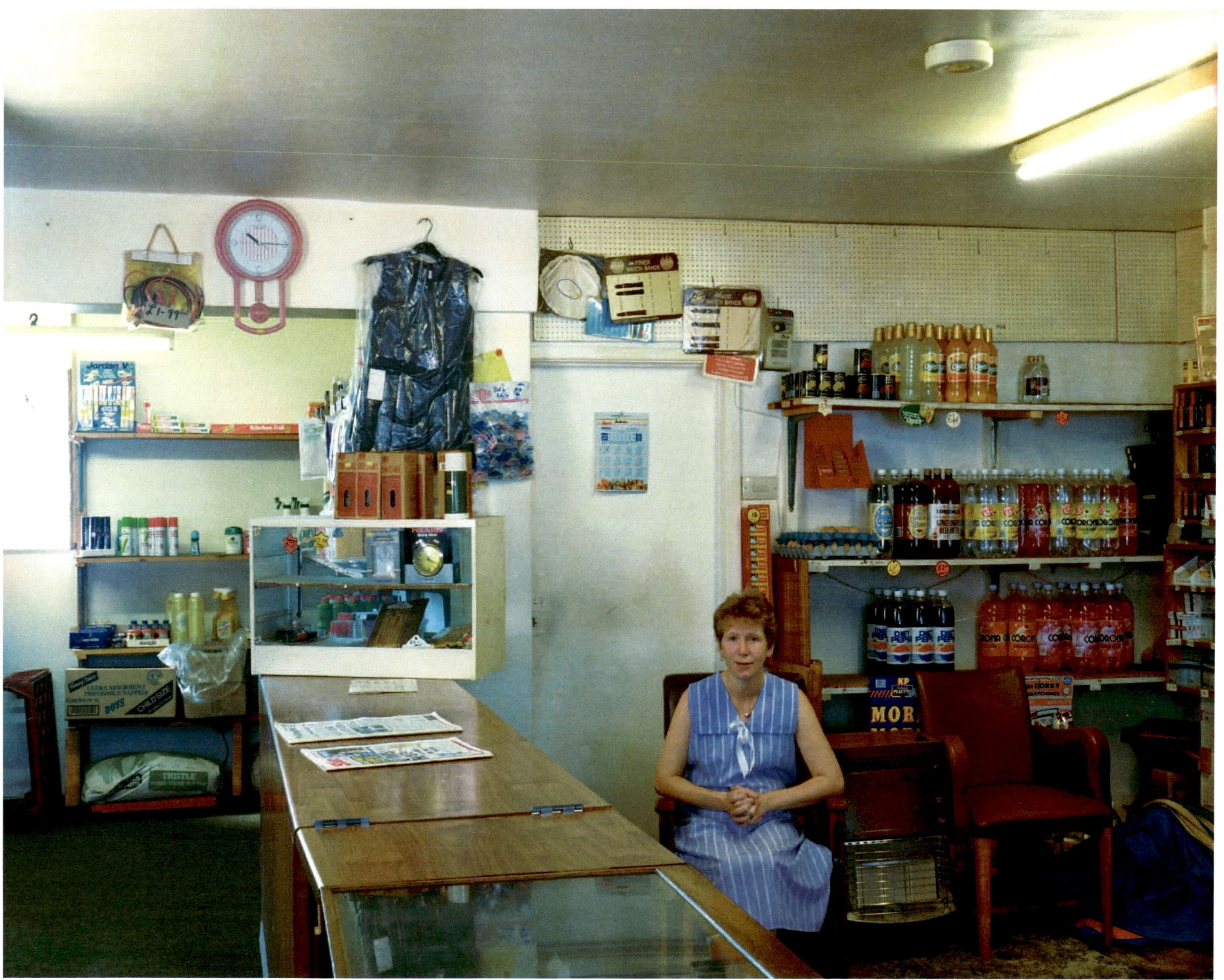

Off License, Croeserw

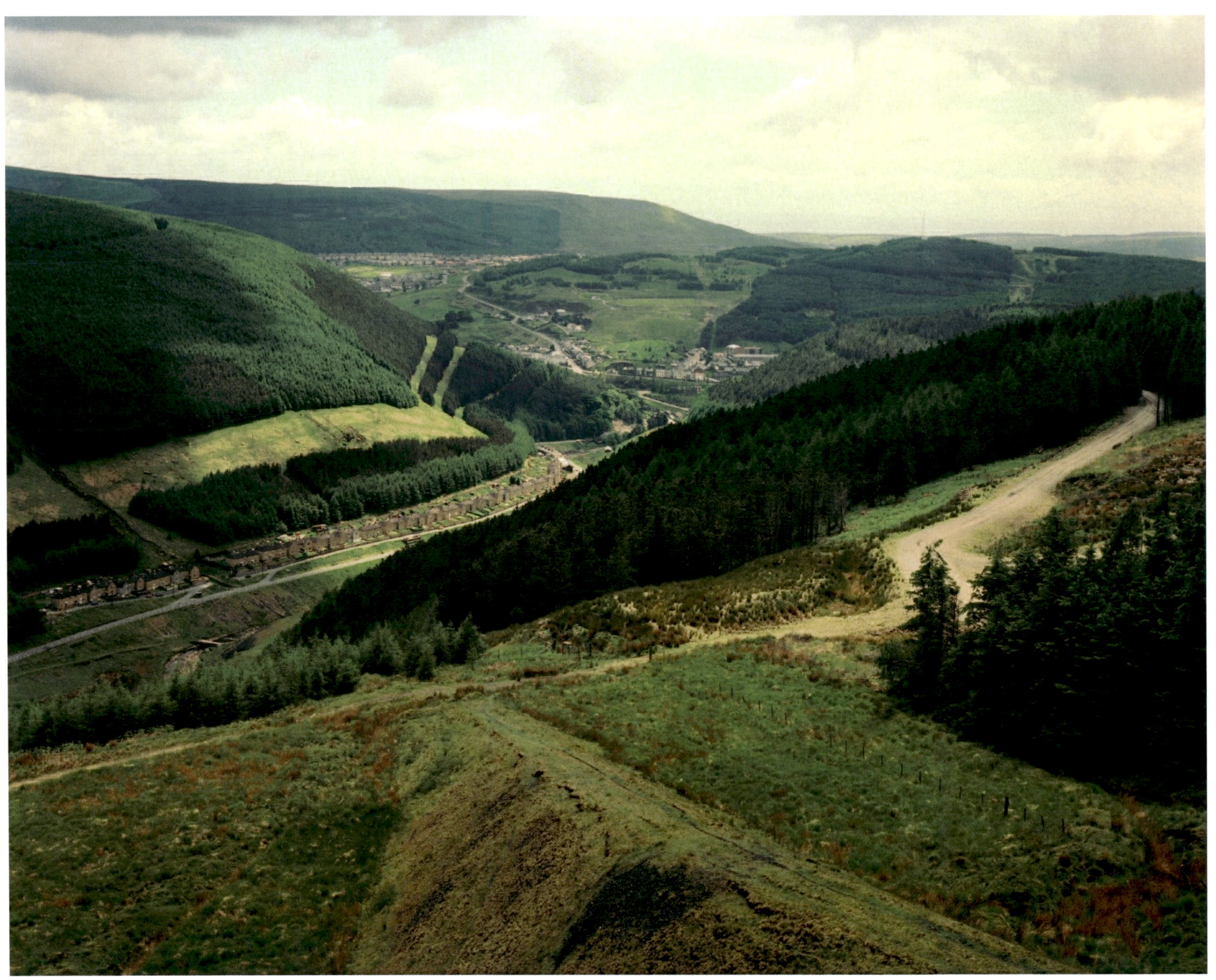

Sunnyside Terrace from Nantwlaeth Colliery, Corrwg Valley

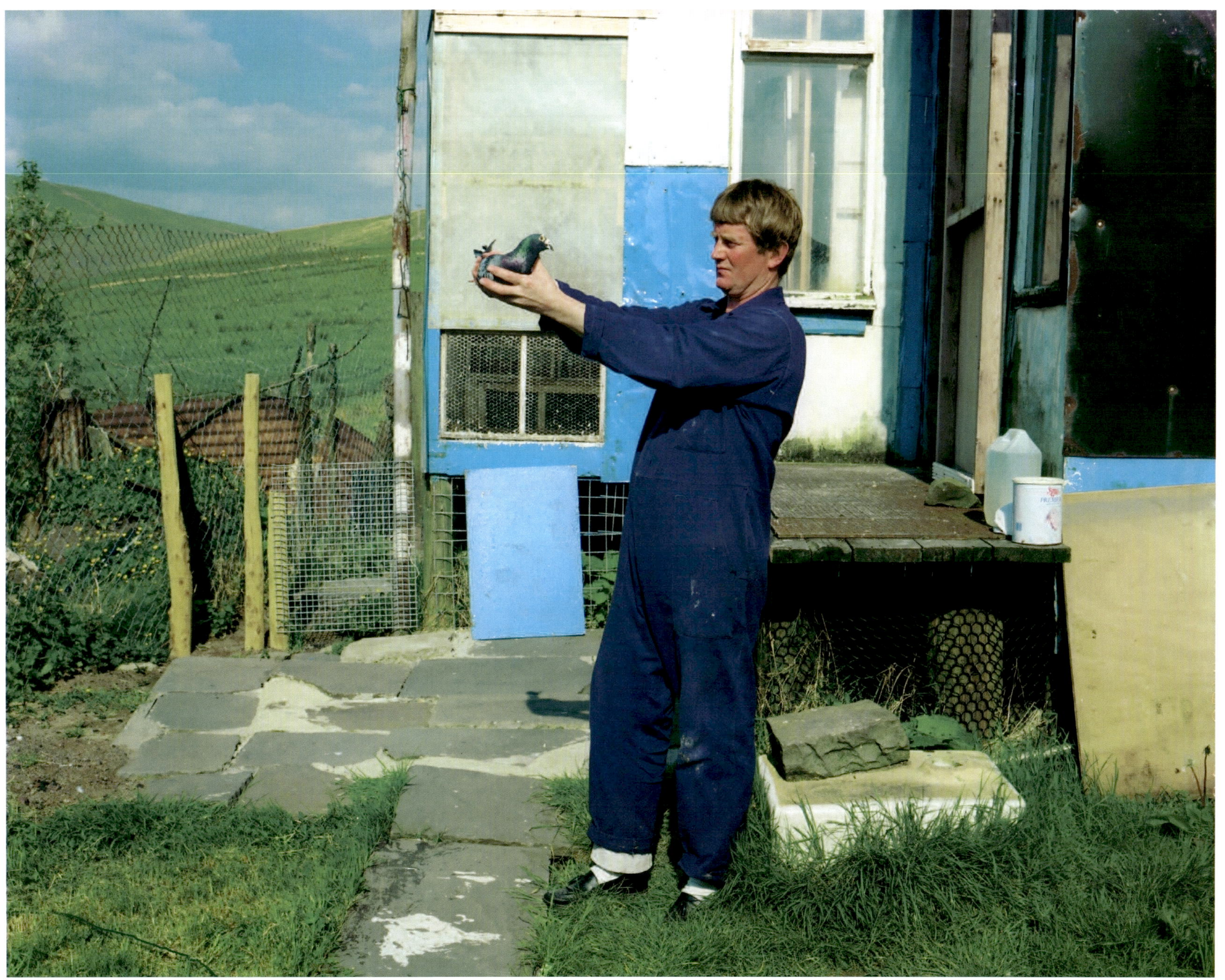

Champion Racing Pigeon, Croeserw

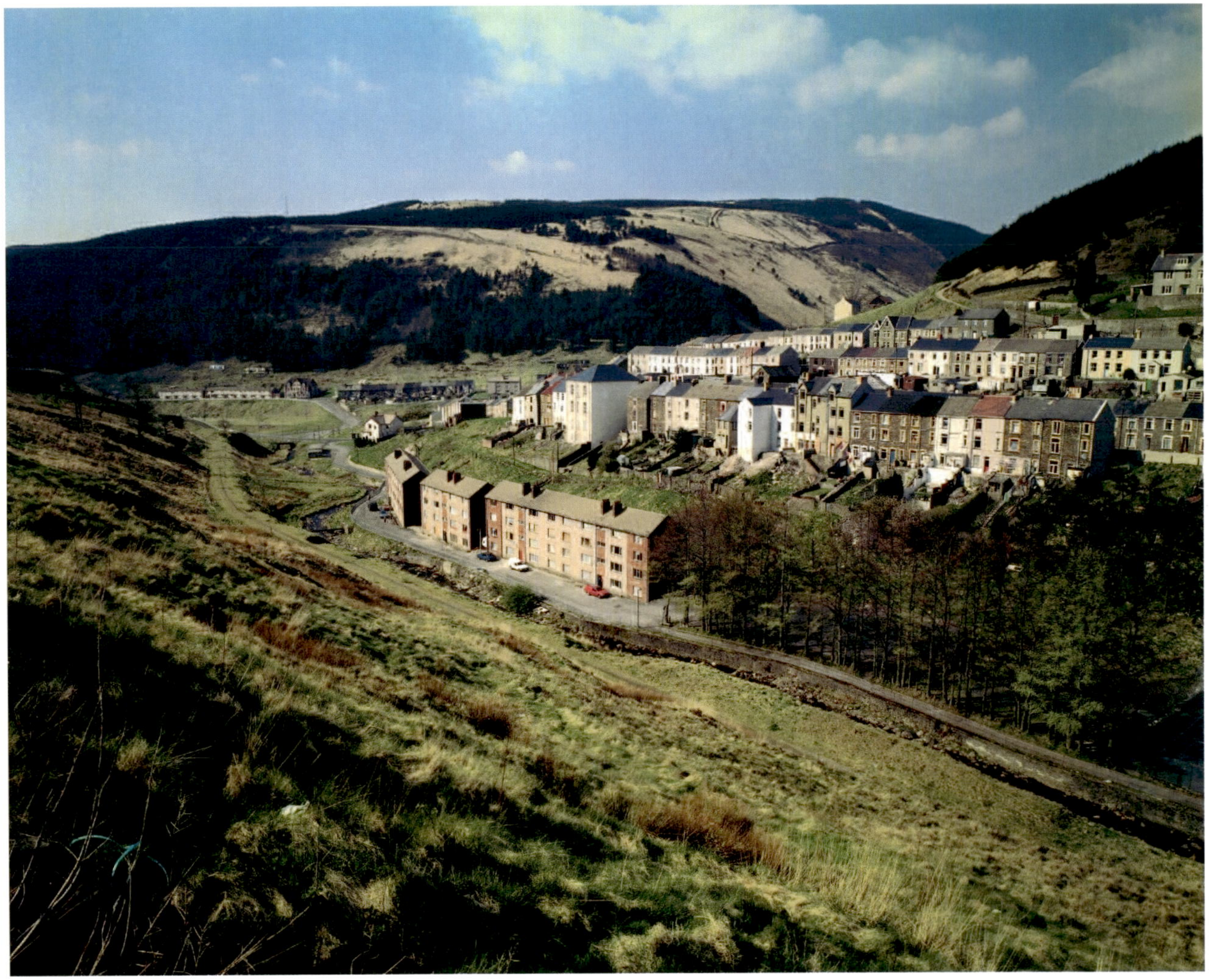

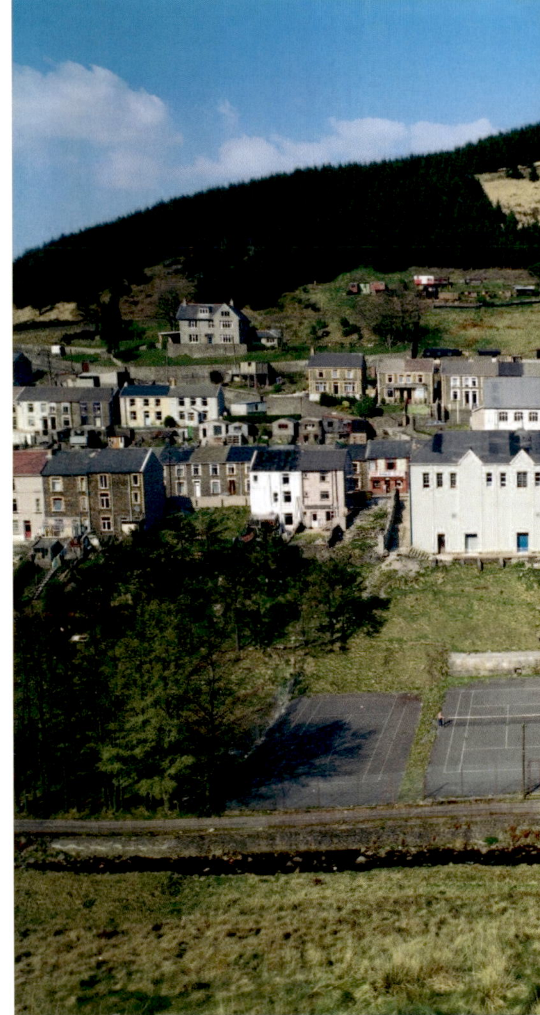

Park Lane Flats

The Gwynfis – 'The Cape'

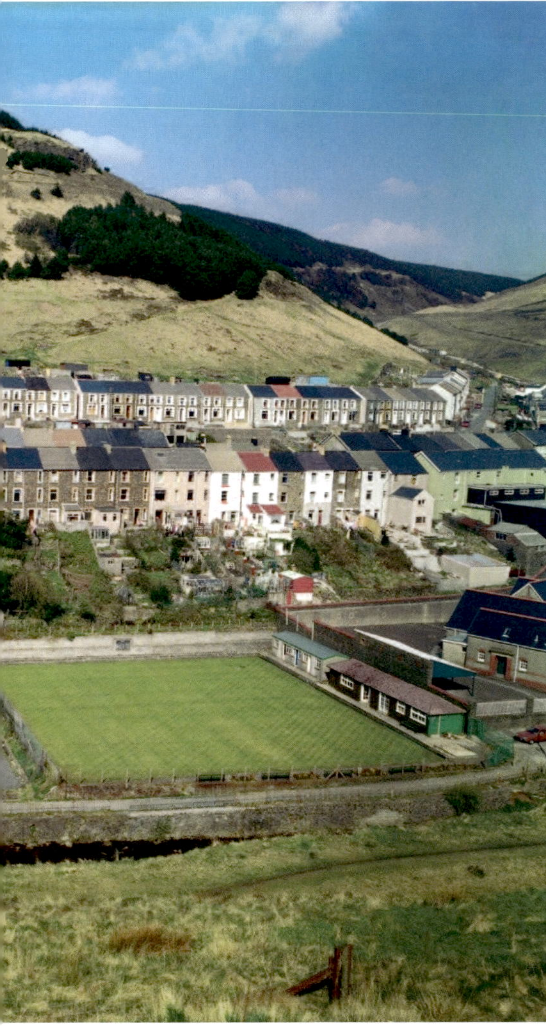

The Miners' Institute

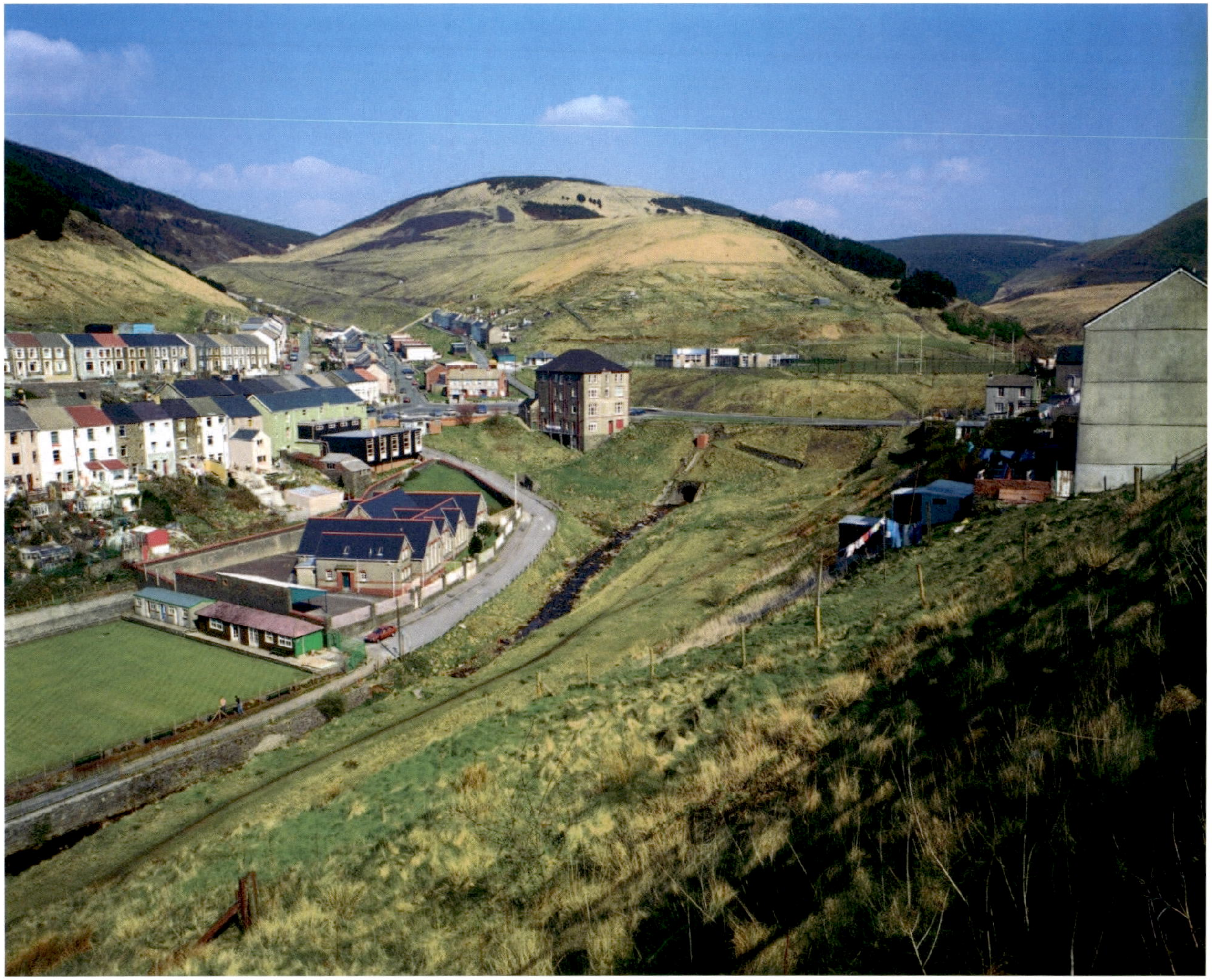

'Great Western'

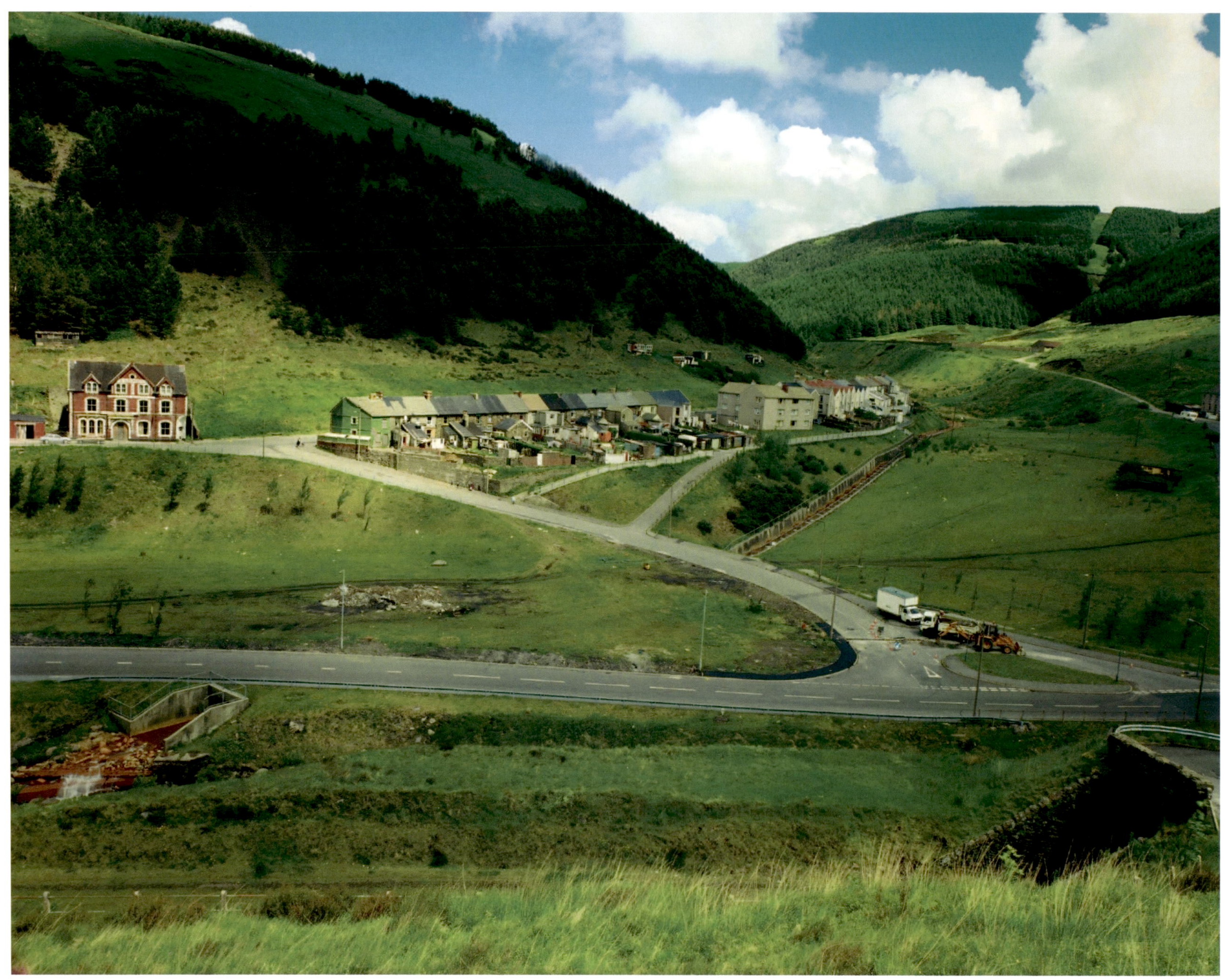

'The Tunnel', Blaengwynfi

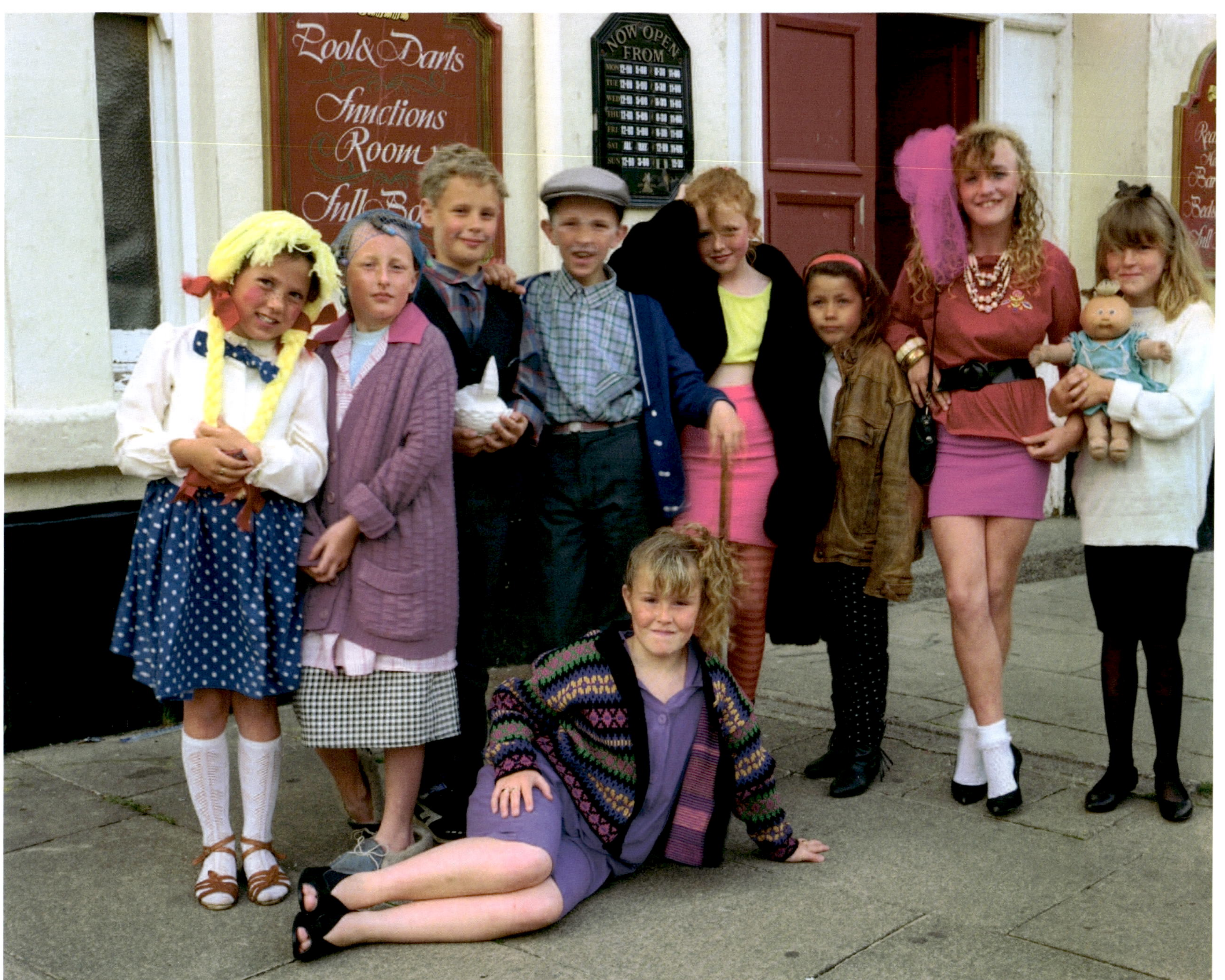

The Cast of 'Bread', Blaengwynfi

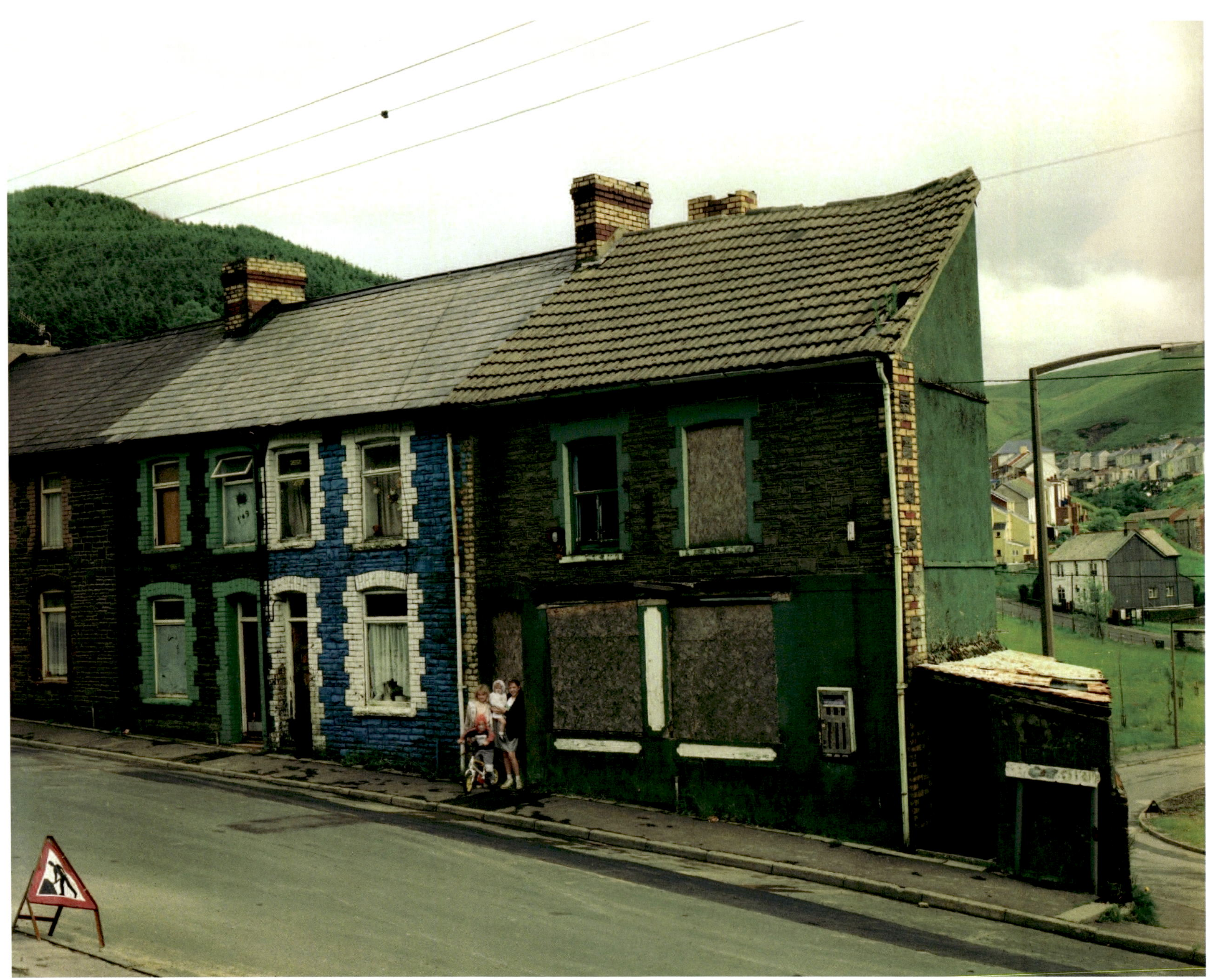

Gwynfi Street, Blaengwynfi

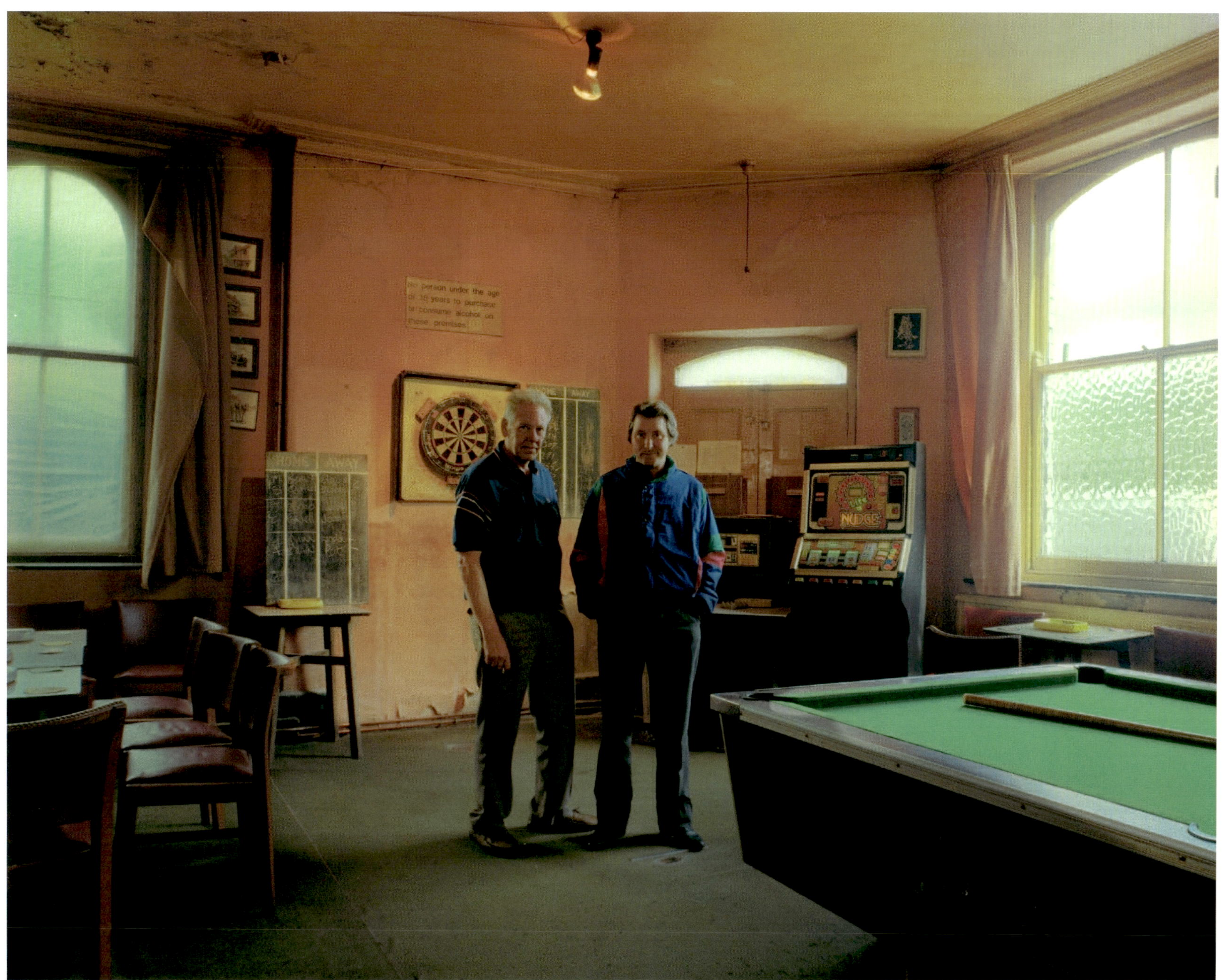

Les & Richie, 'The Tunnel', Blaengwynfi

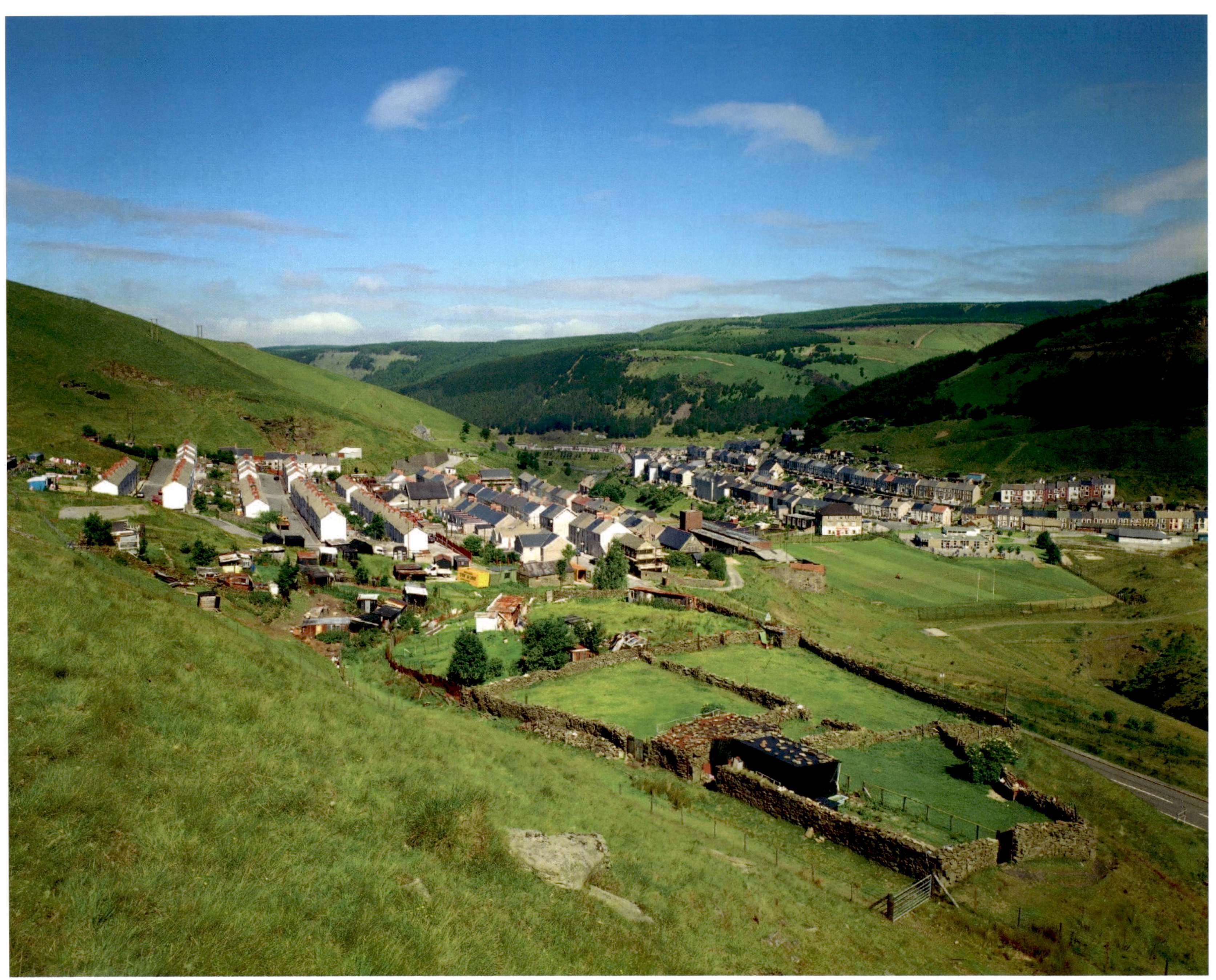

Site of Afan Colliery, Abergwynfi
(Now school playing field)

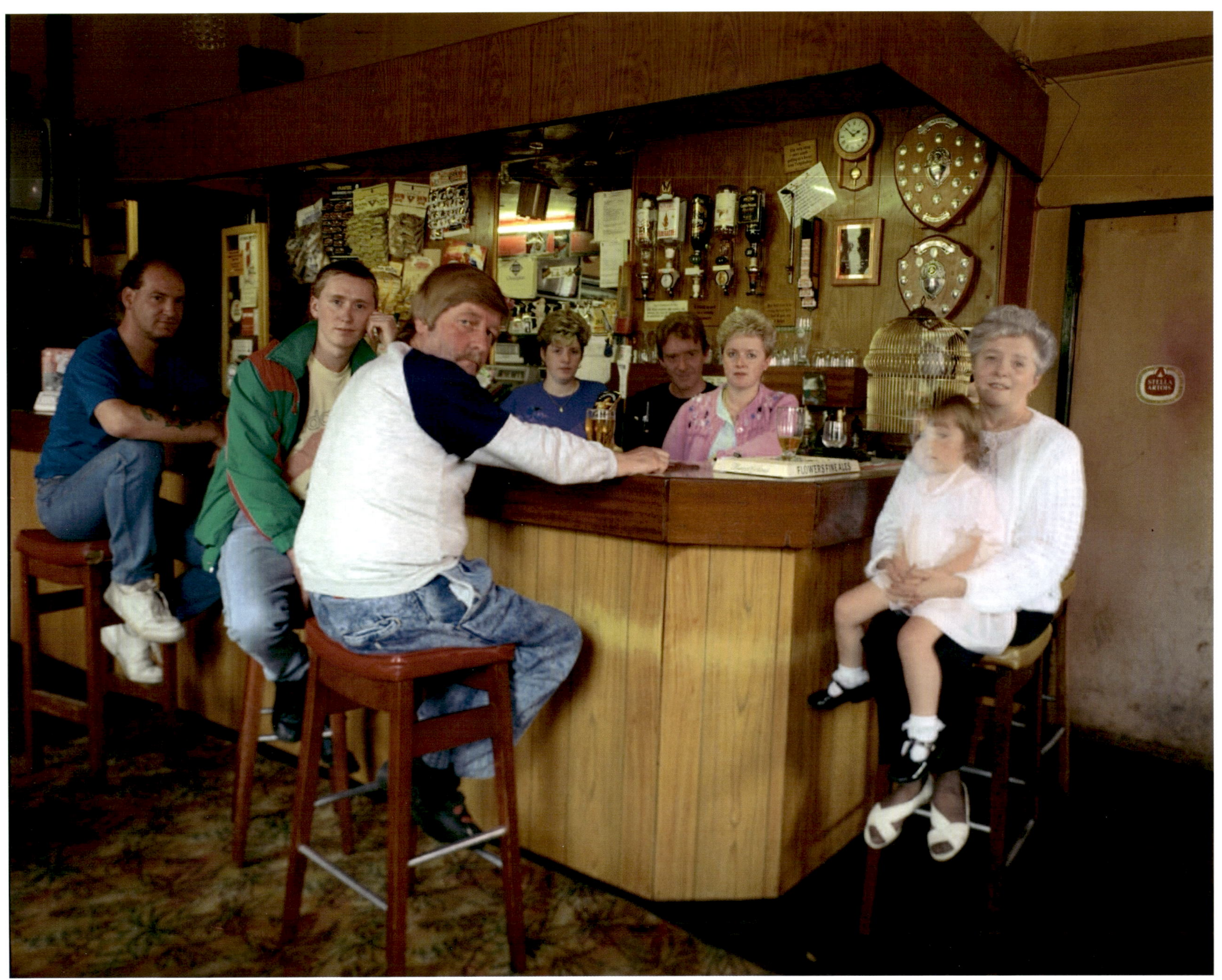

'Great Western', Blaengwynfi

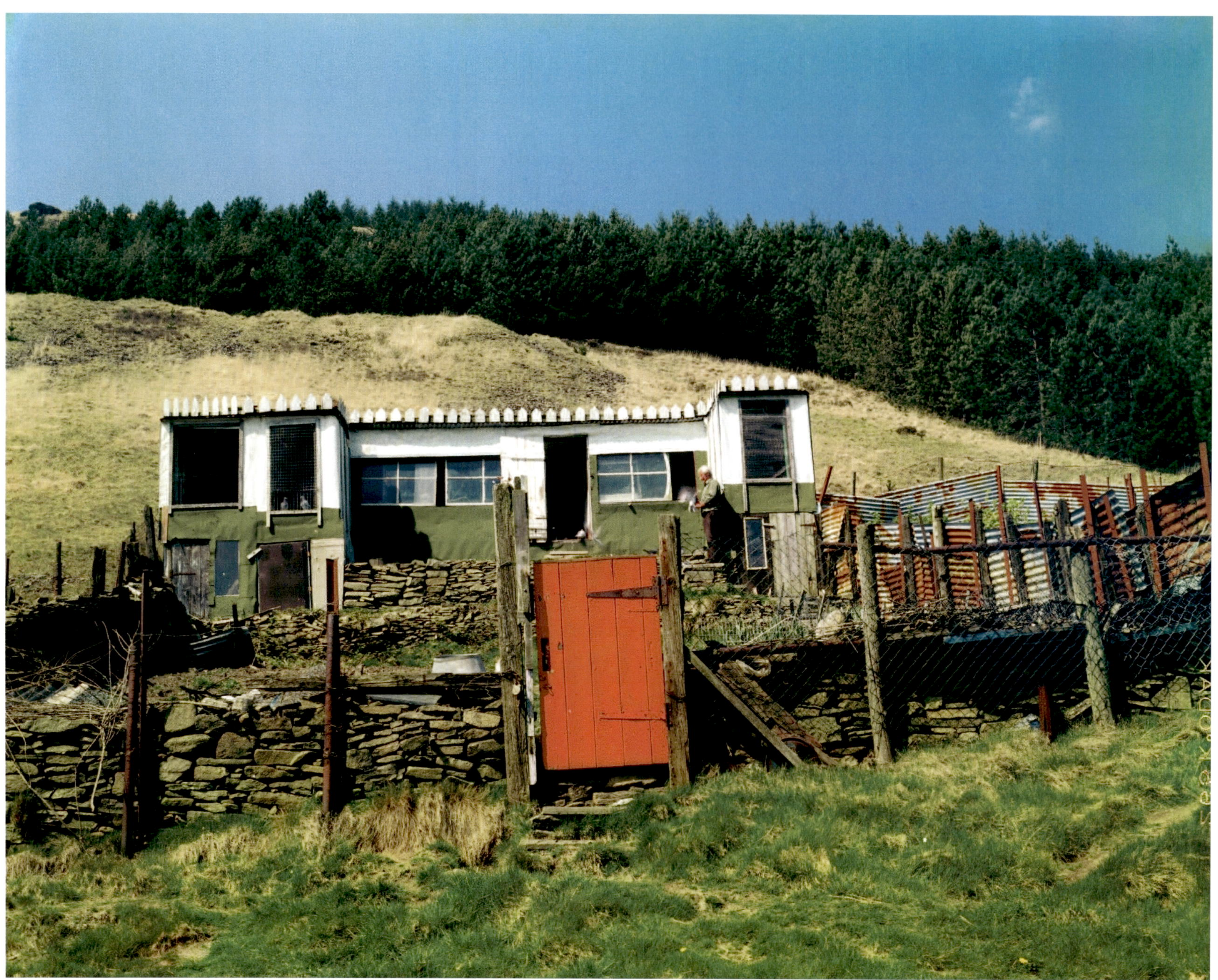

Pigeon Palace, Blaengwynfi

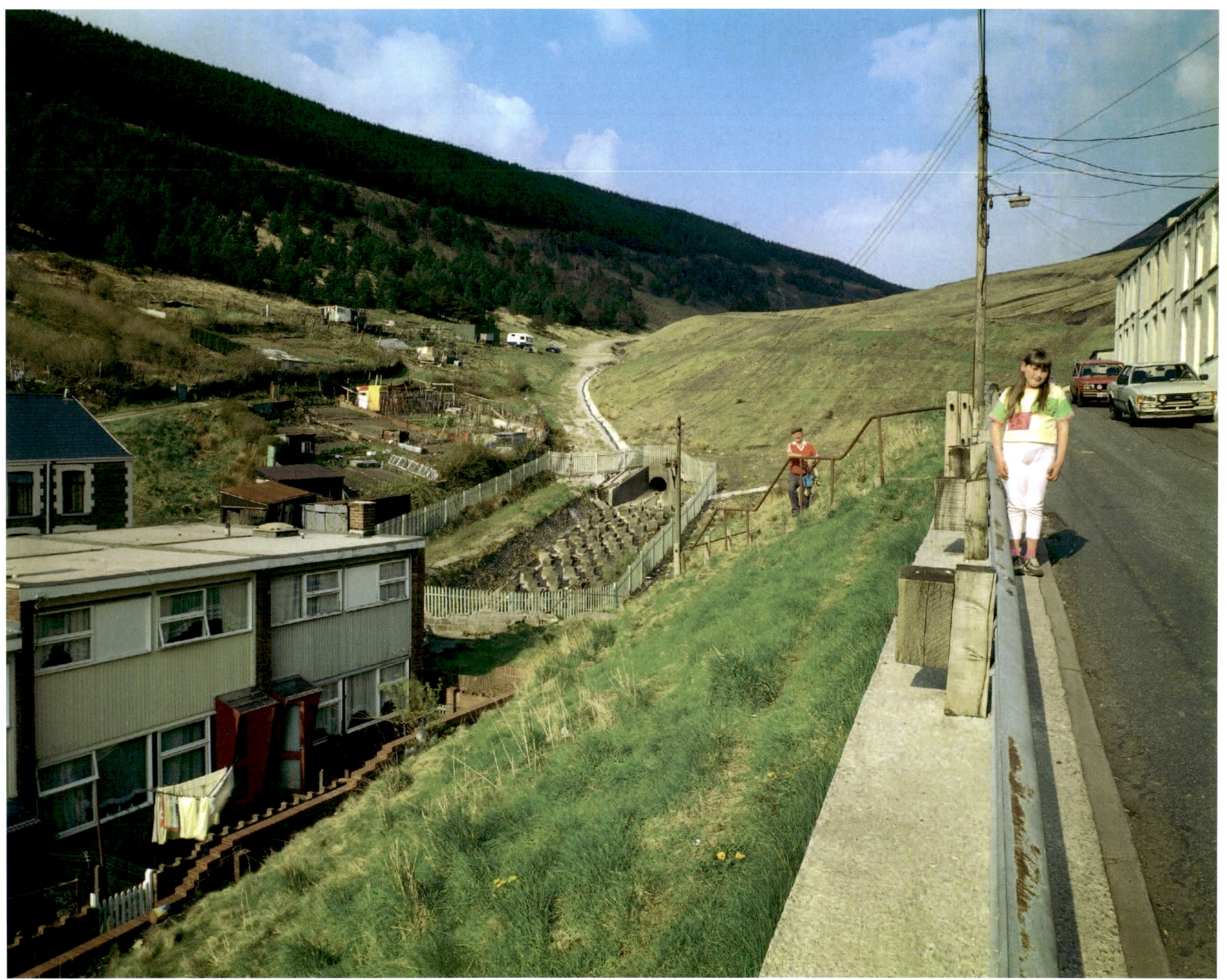

Outfall, Blaengwynfi

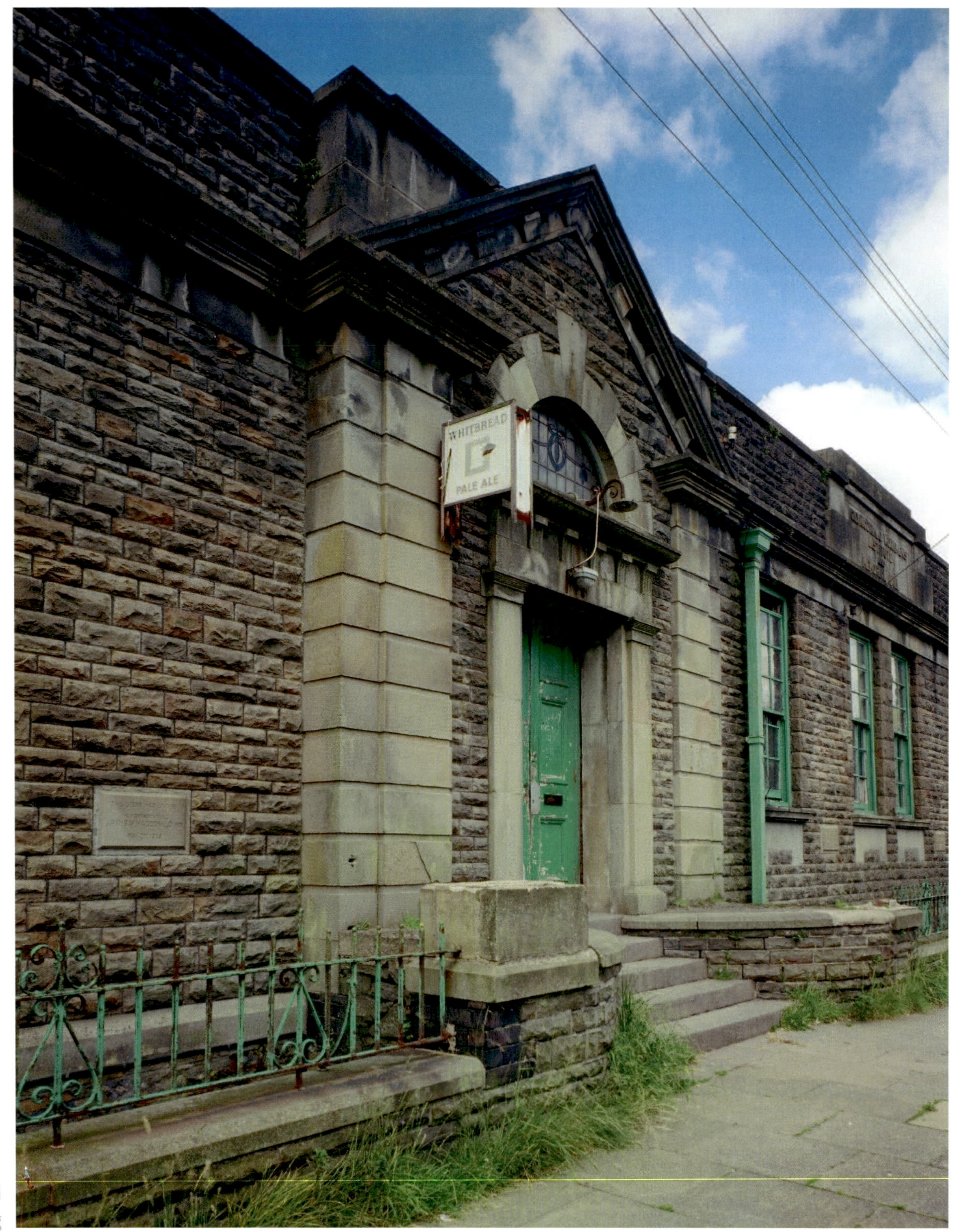

Miners' Welfare Hall
Glyncorrwg

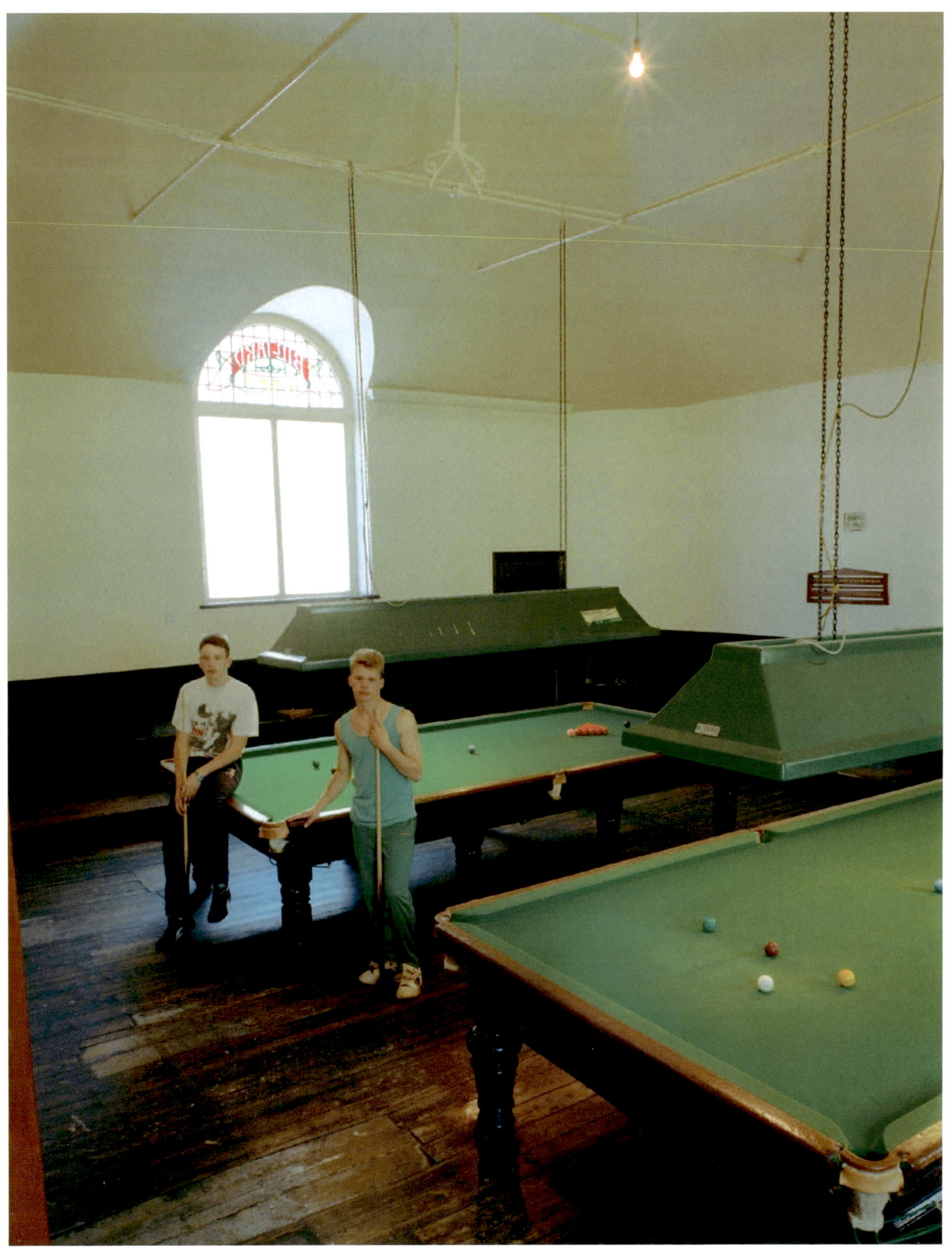

Billiard Room
Miners' Institute
Blaengwynfi

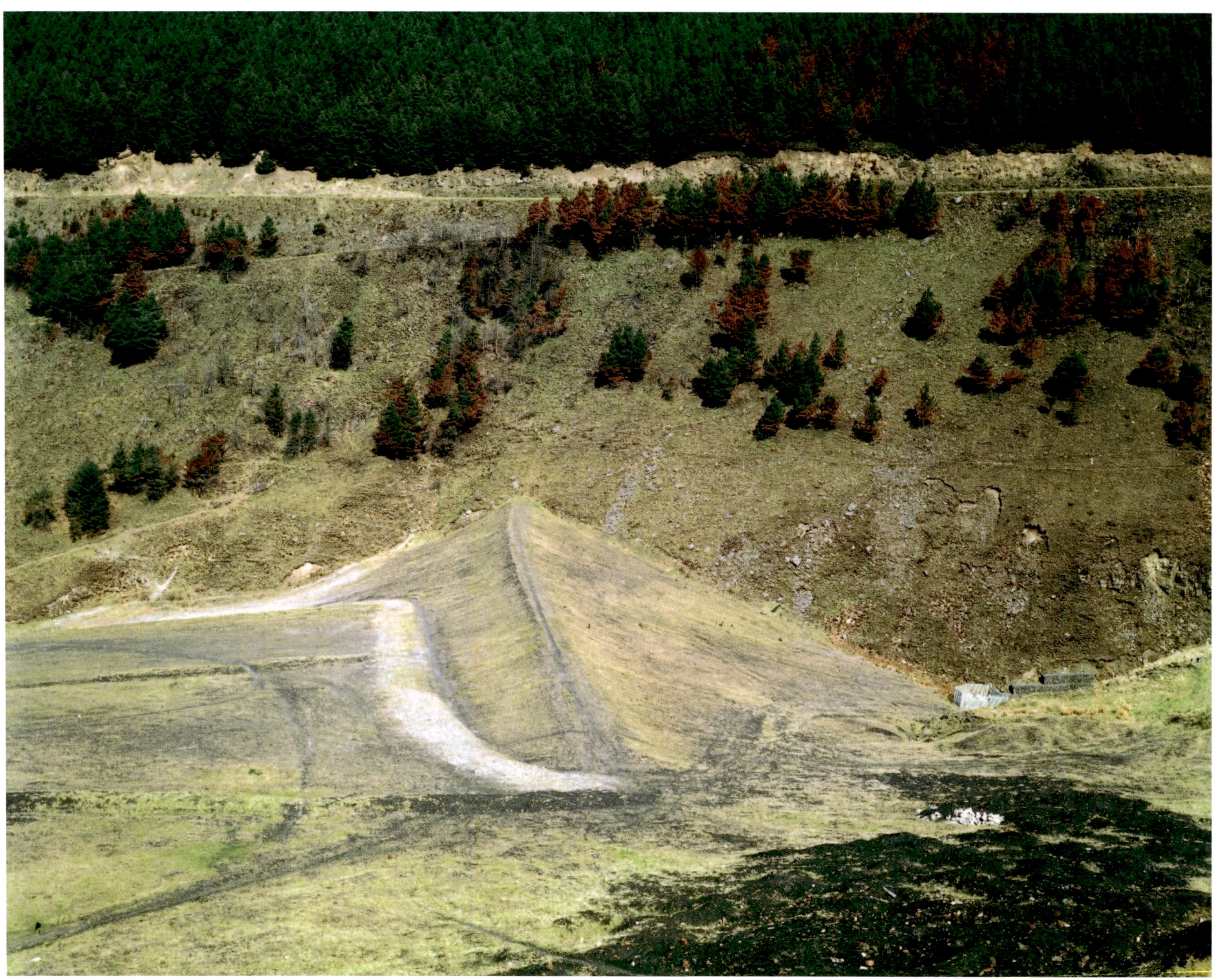

Nantgwyn, Blaengwynfi

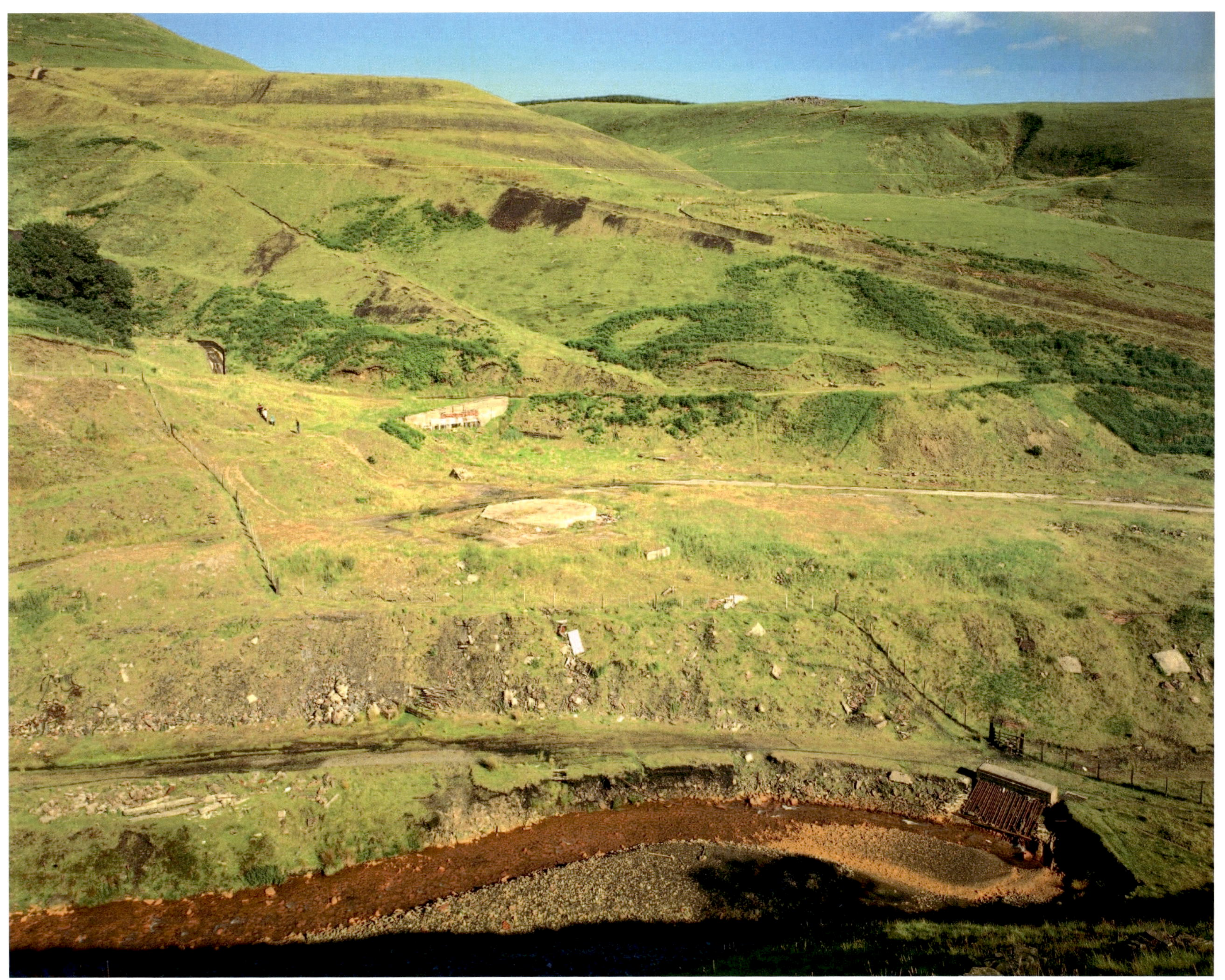

Capped Shaft on Site of South Pit, Glyncorrwg

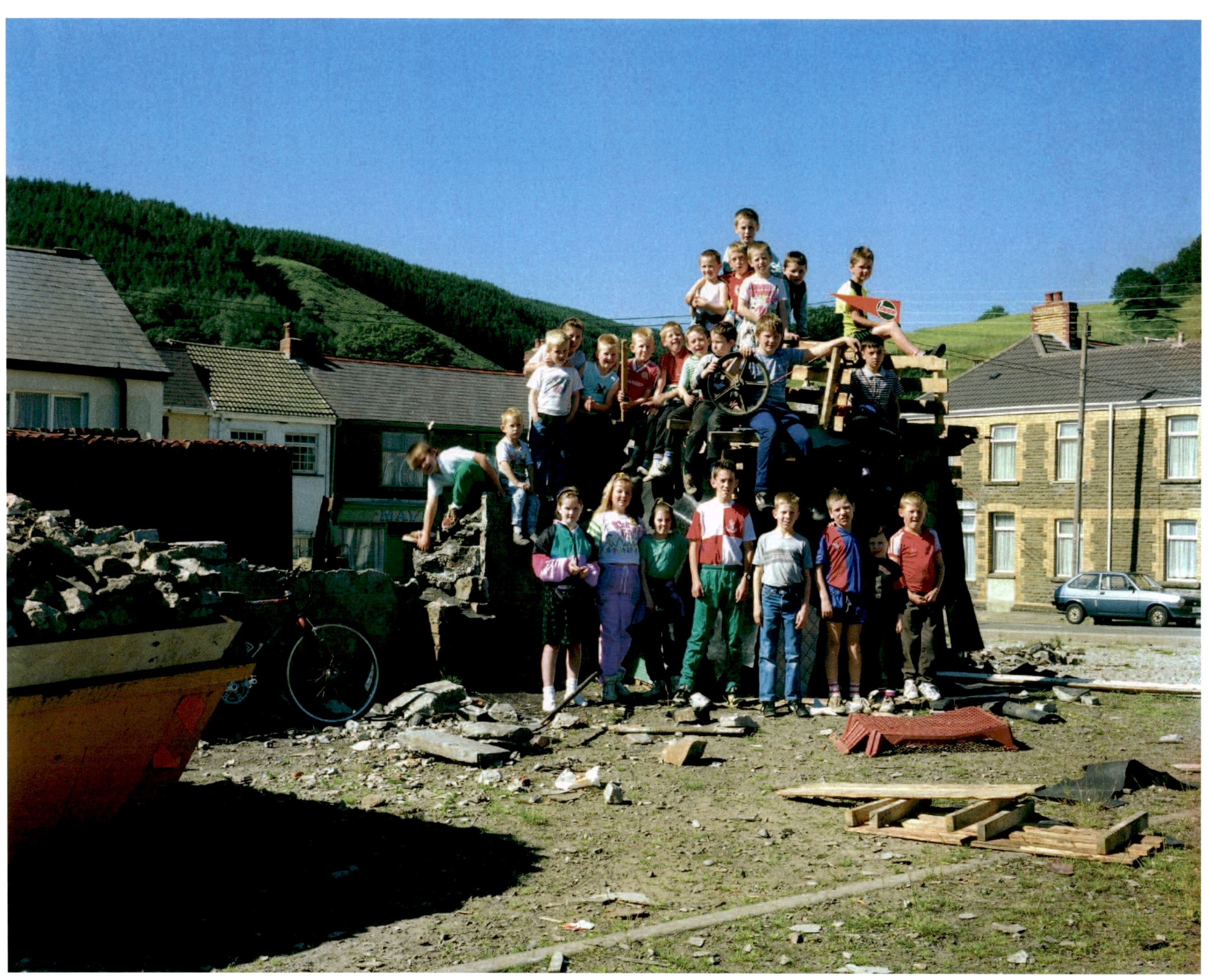

Children's Camp, The Square, Glyncorrwg

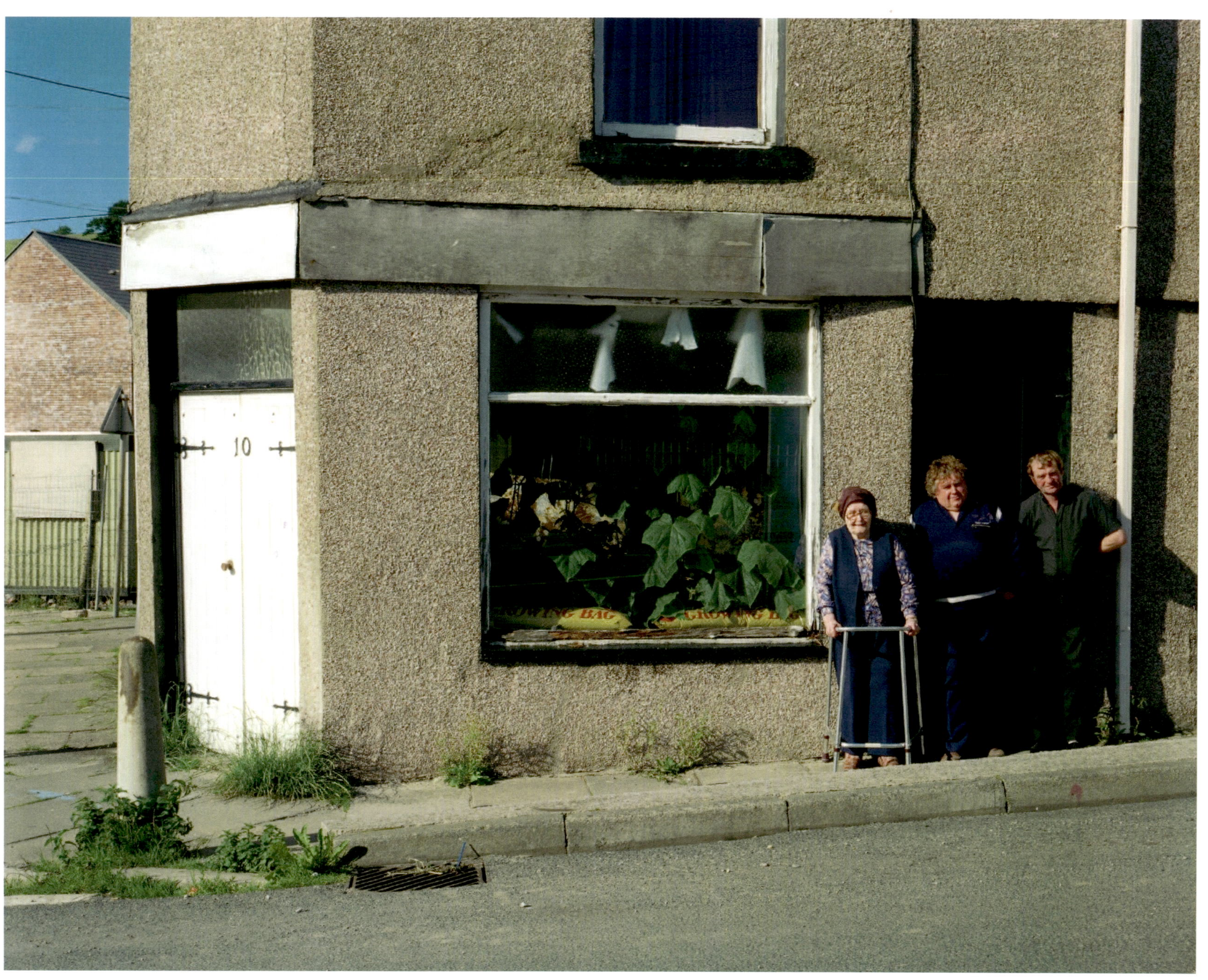

Cucumbers, Bridge Street, Glyncorrwg

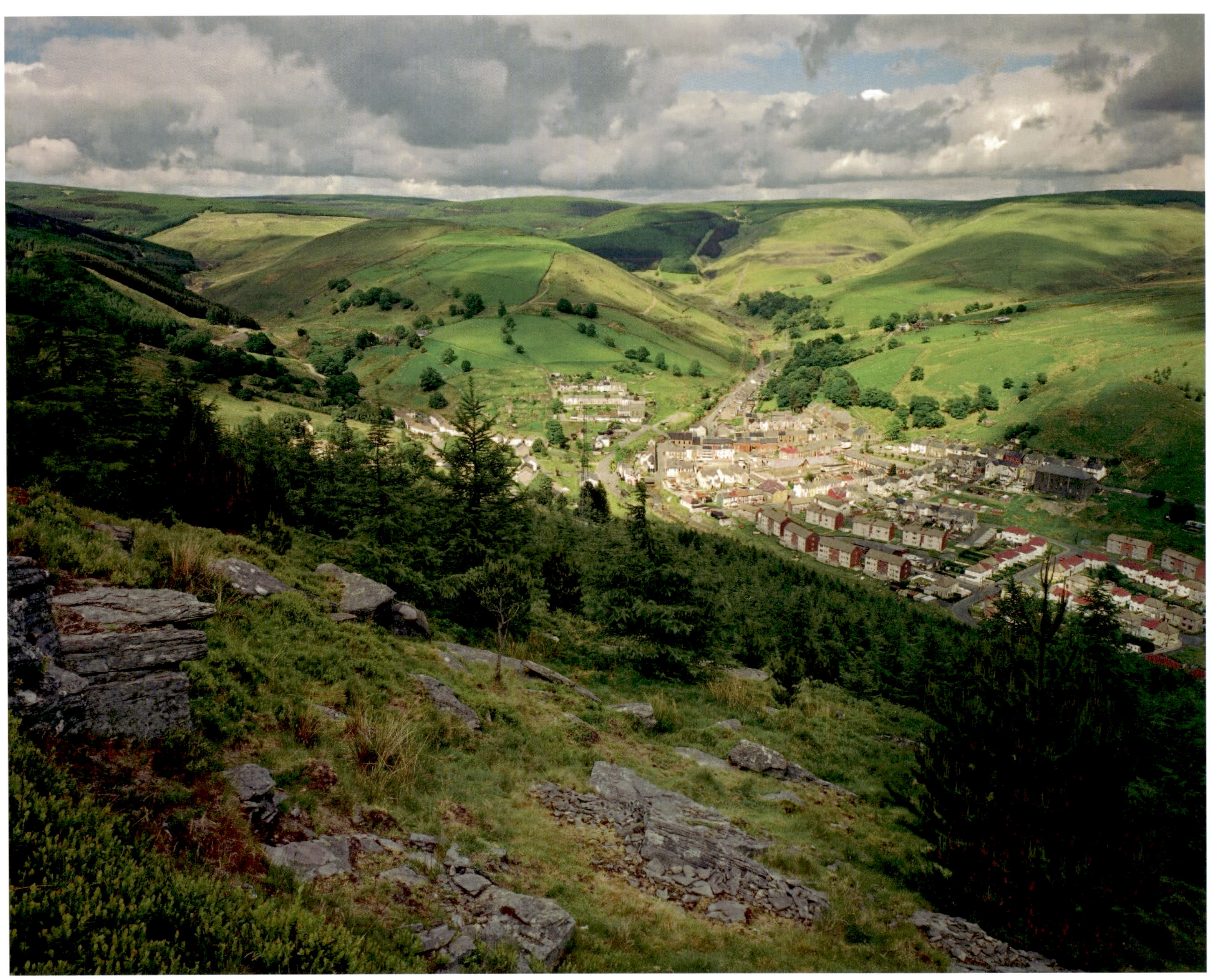

Sites of North & South Pits
(In valleys behind Glyncorrwg)

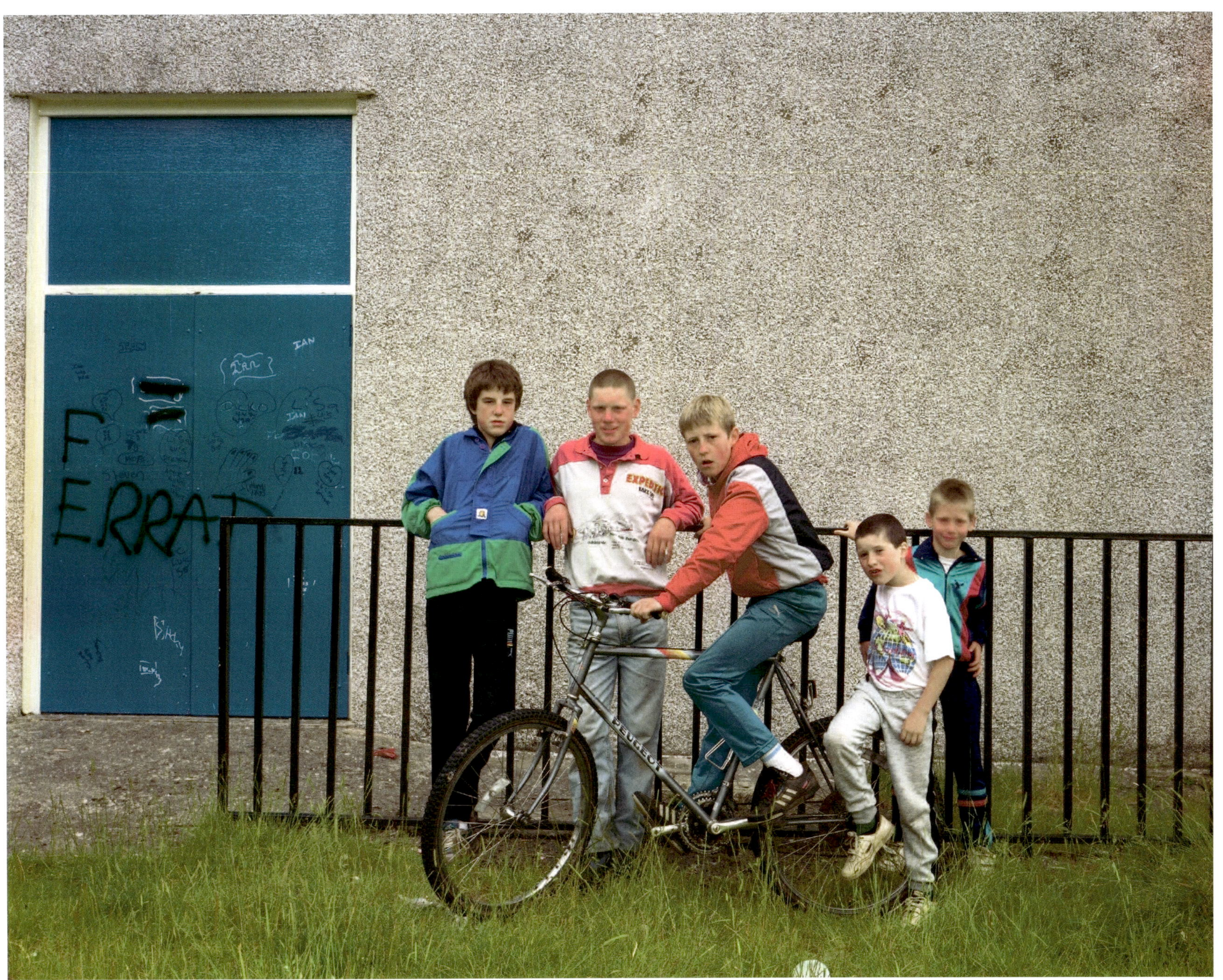

'Ferrat' and Friends, Glyncorrwg

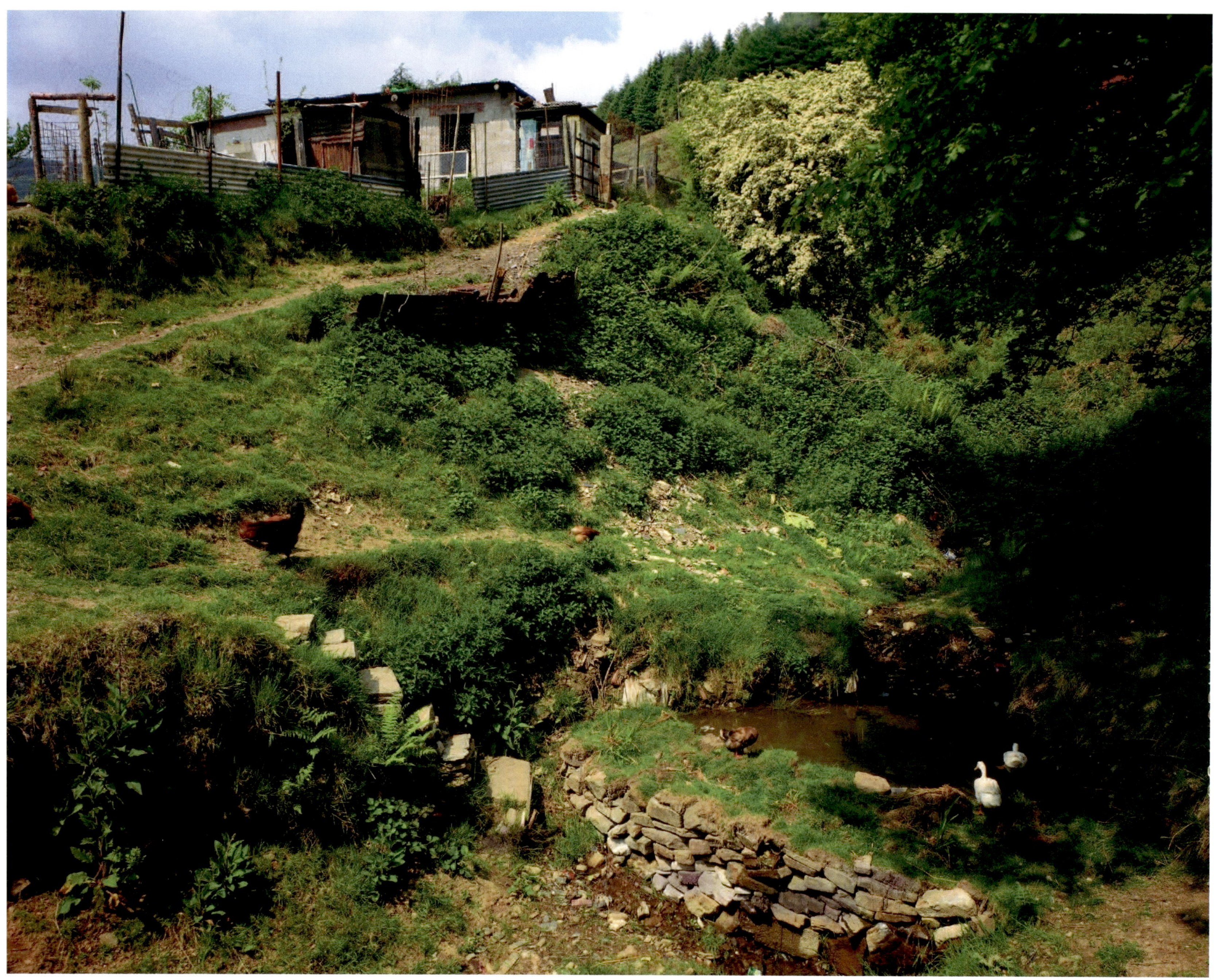

Pond, Abercregan

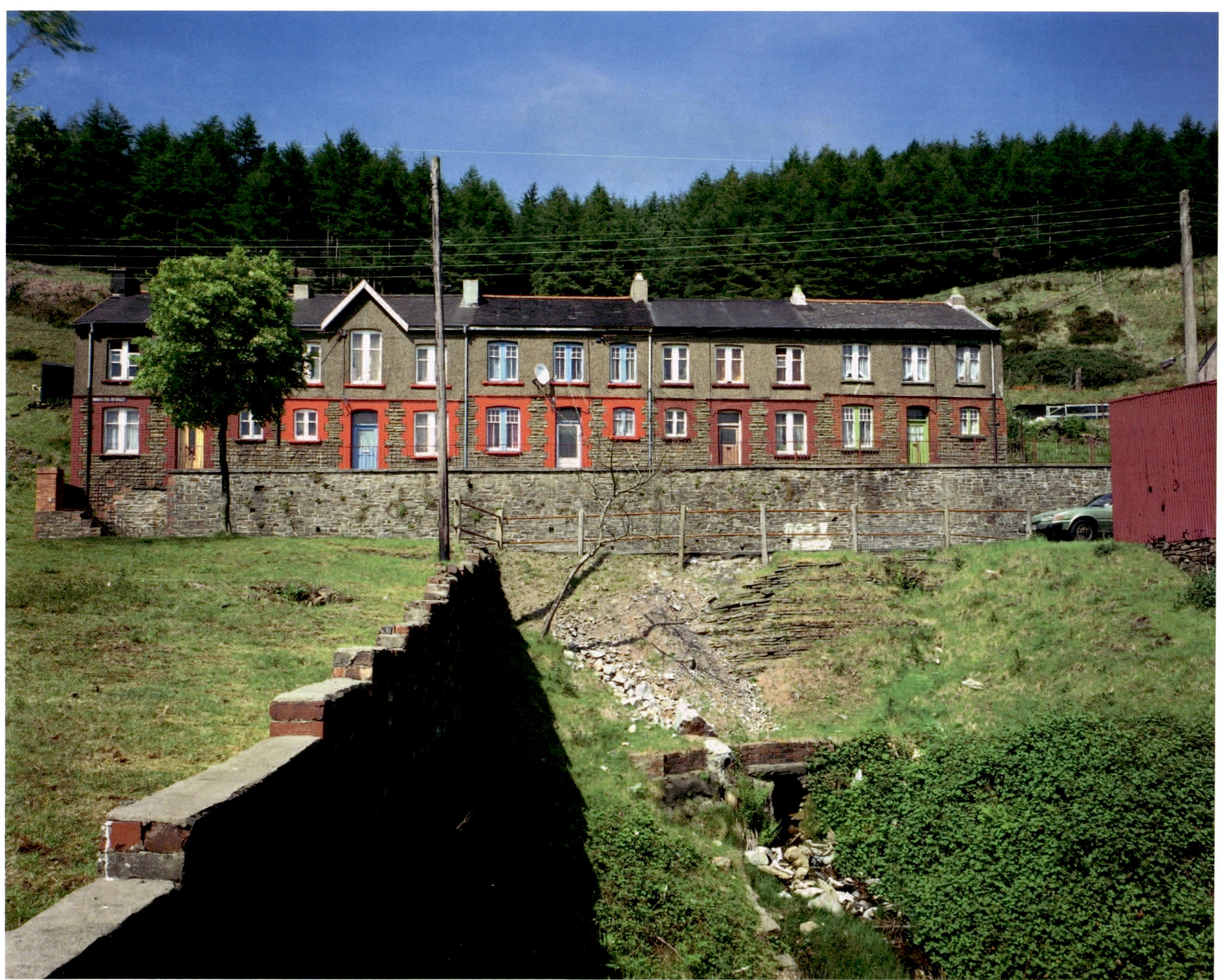

Remains of Prosser's Terrace, Abercregan

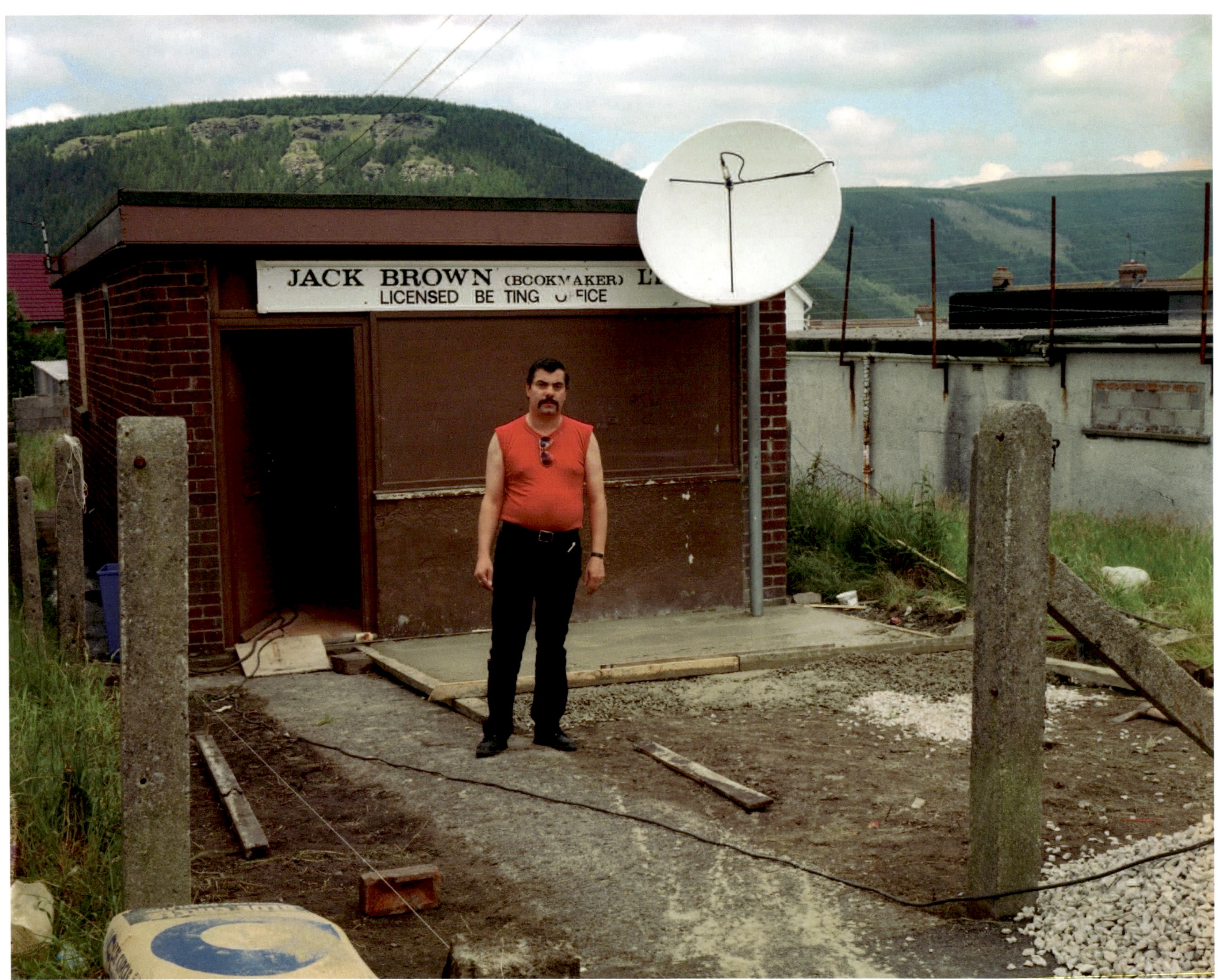

Tony, Betting Shop, Croeserw

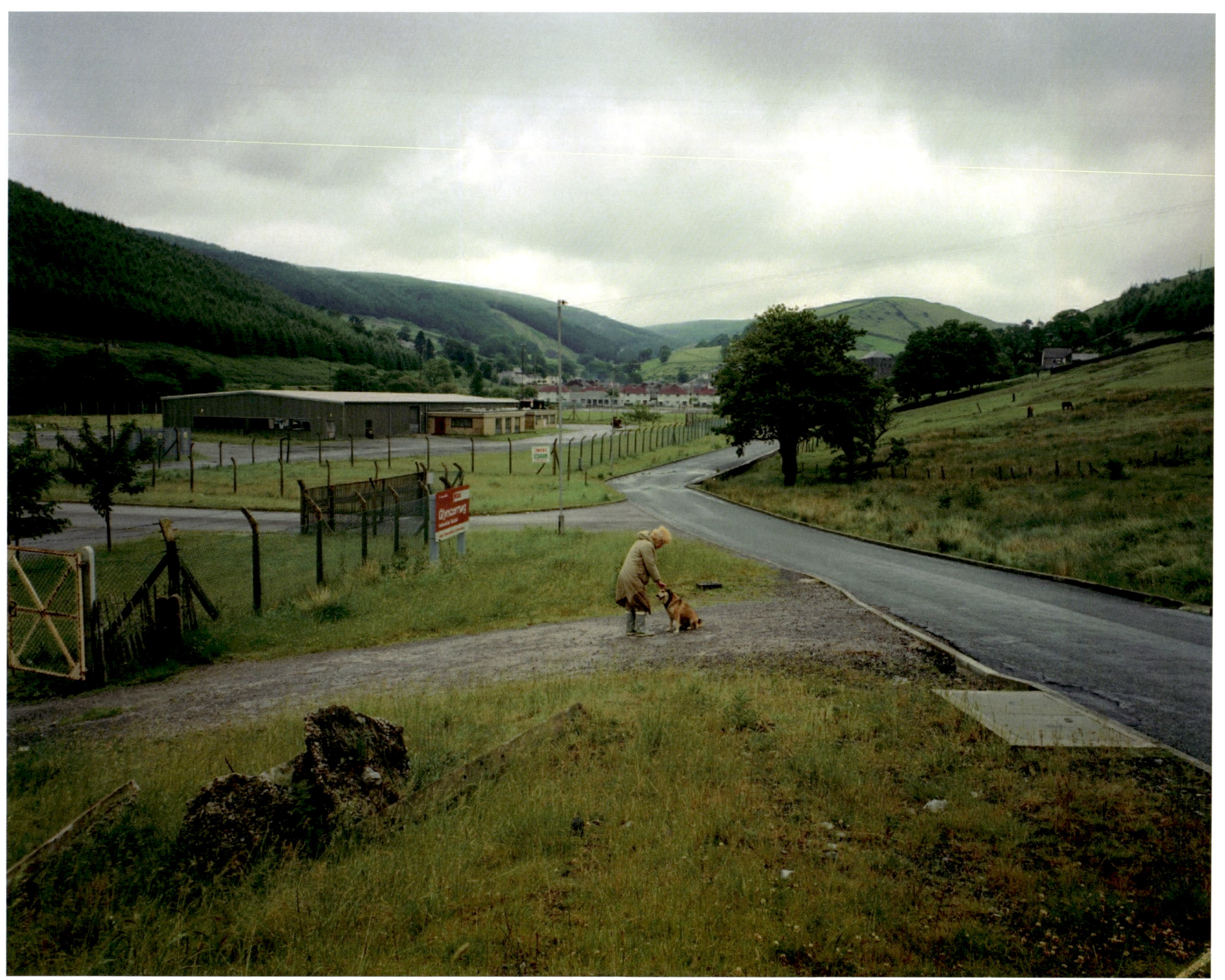

'Freeway' the Dog, Industrial Estate, Glyncorrwg

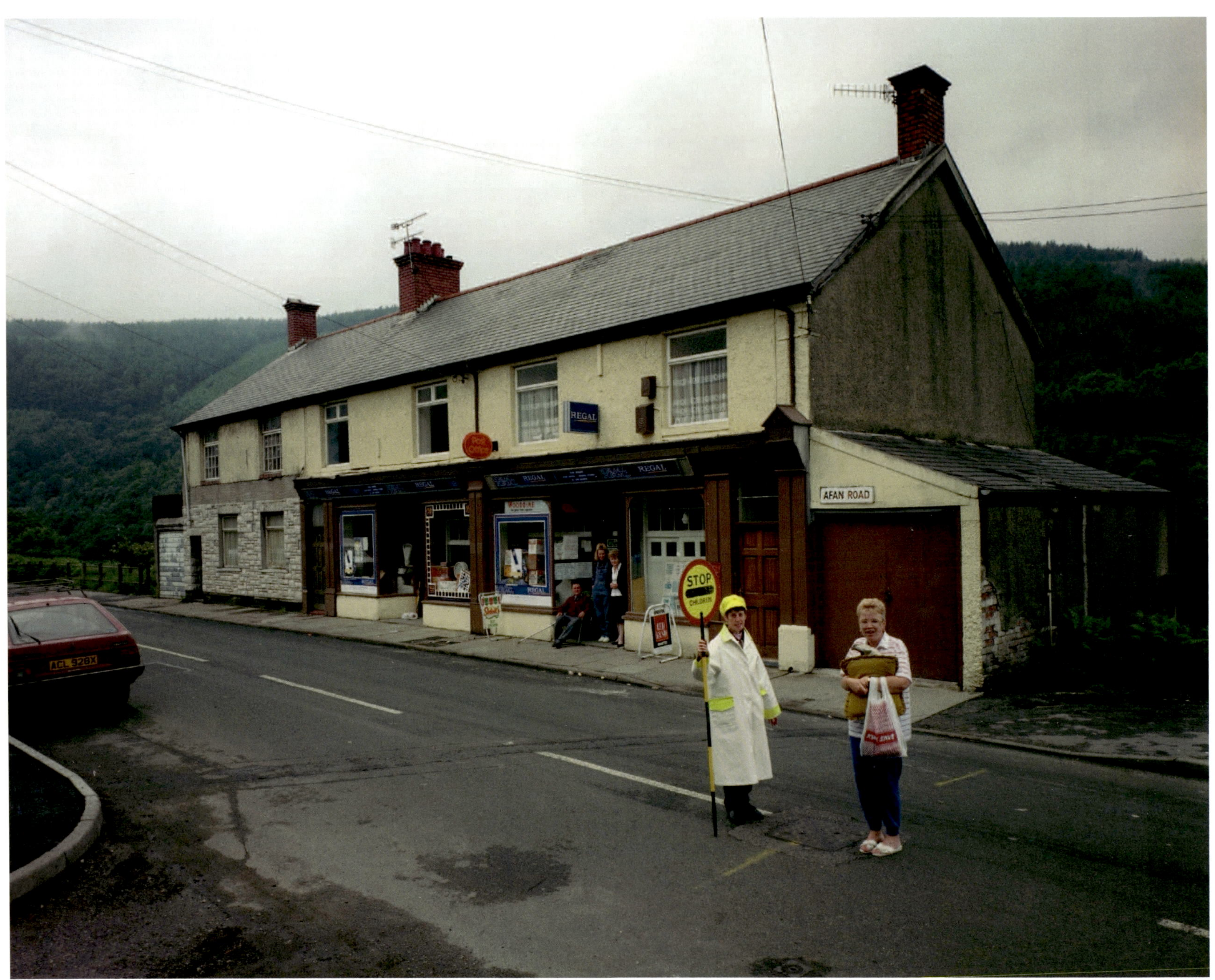

Post Office, Afan Road, Duffryn

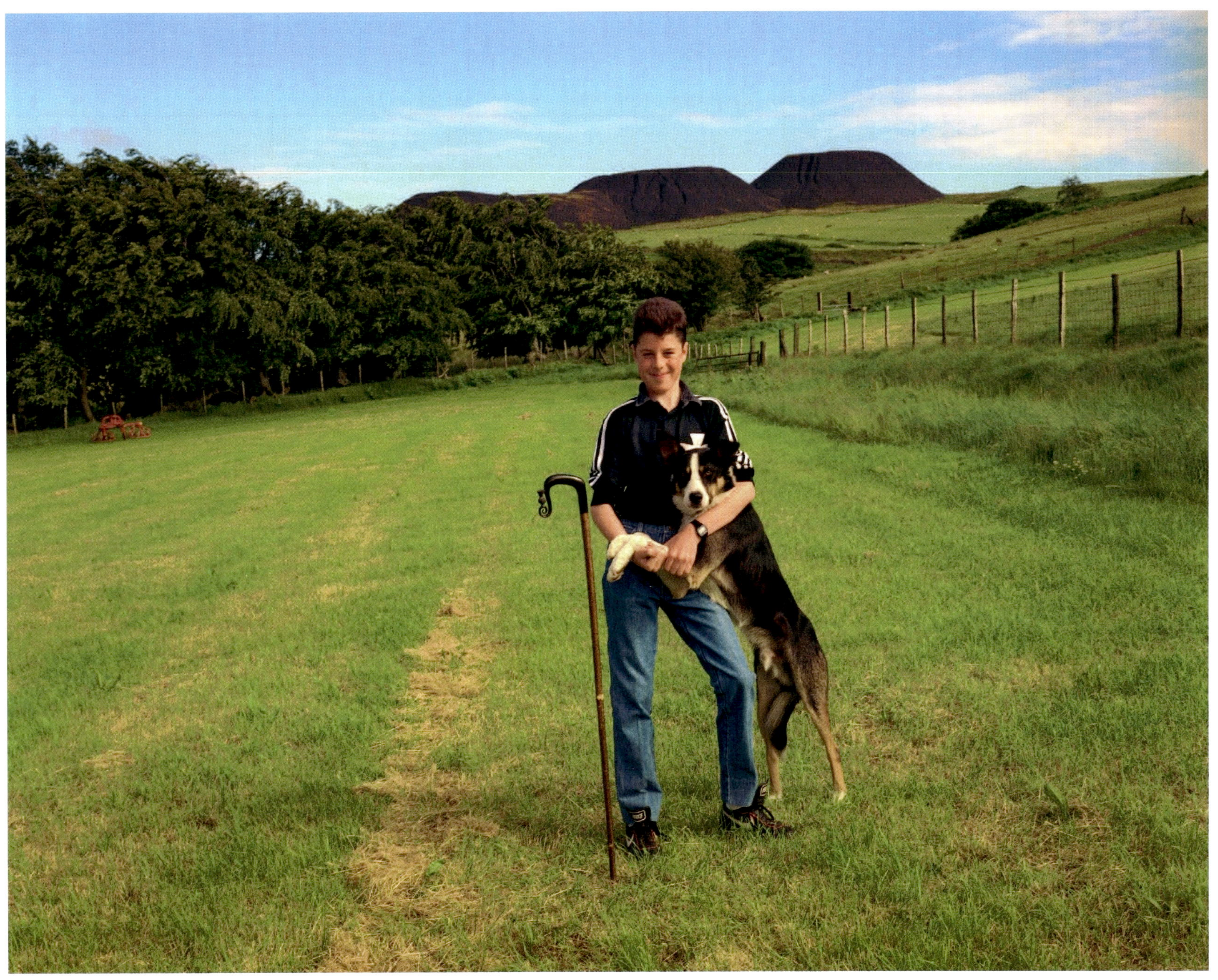

Robert and 'Roy', Dyffryn

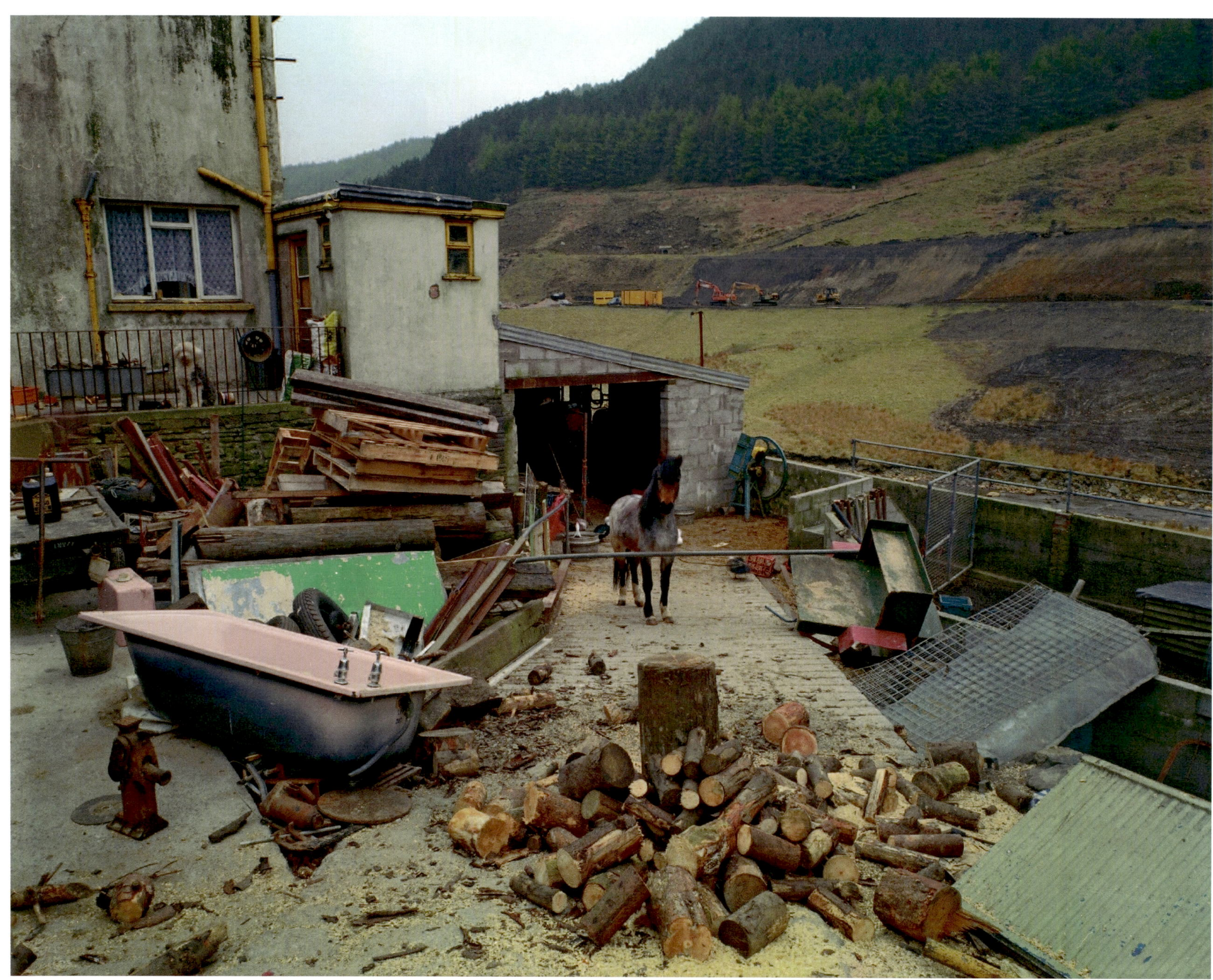

Sunnyside Terrace, Corrwg Valley

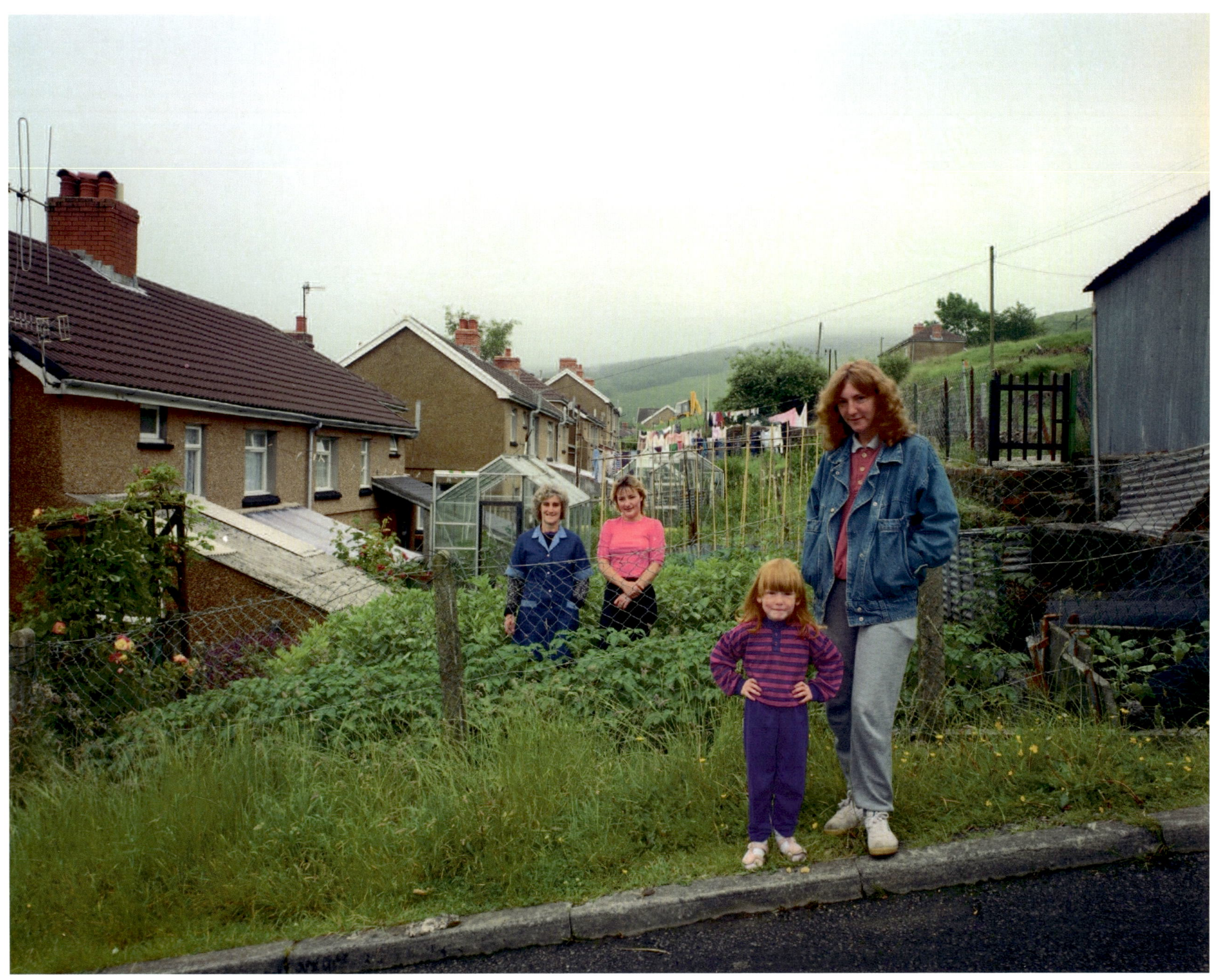

Back Gardens, Duffryn

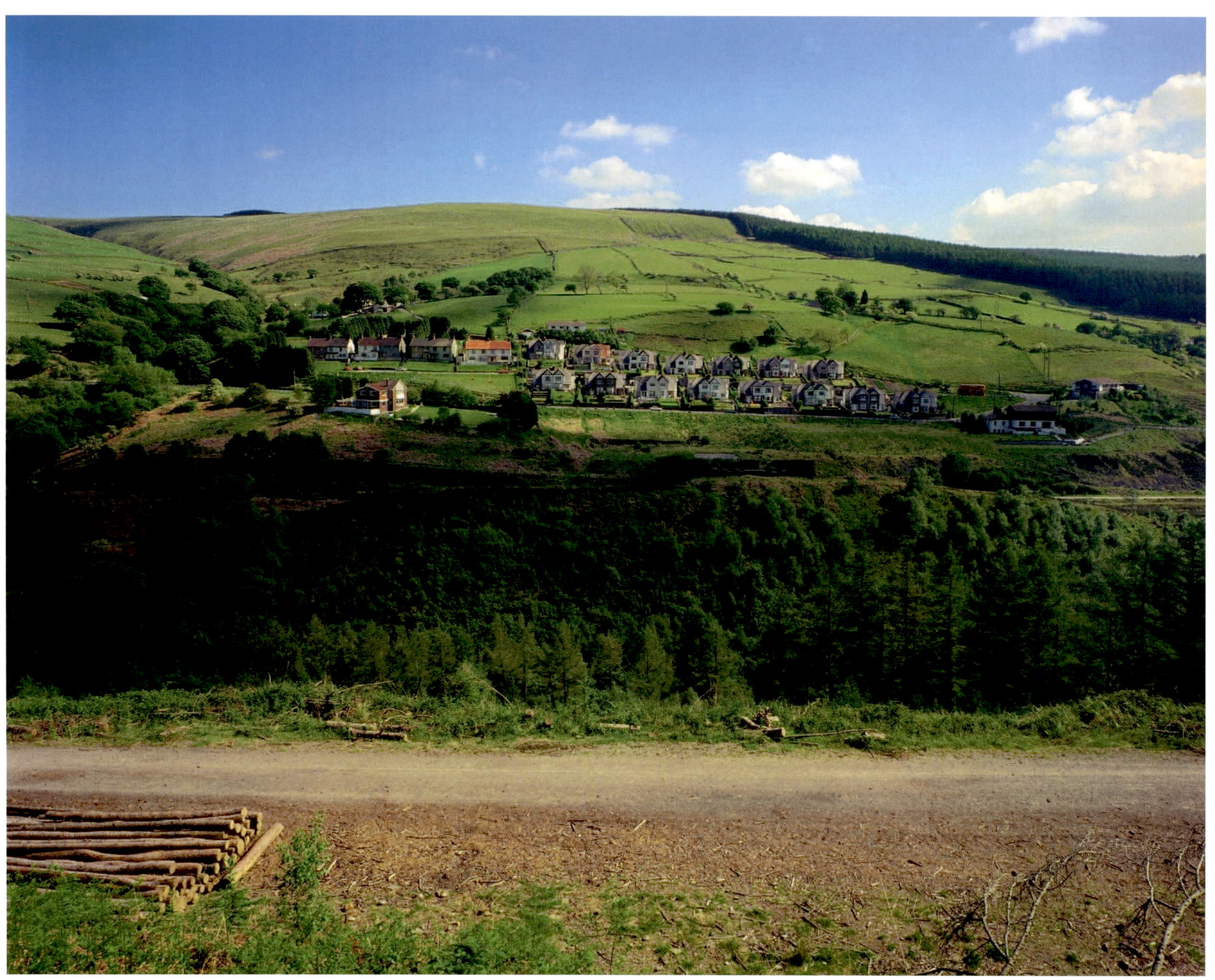

Colliery Managers' Houses, Cynonville
(Overlooking site of colliery.)

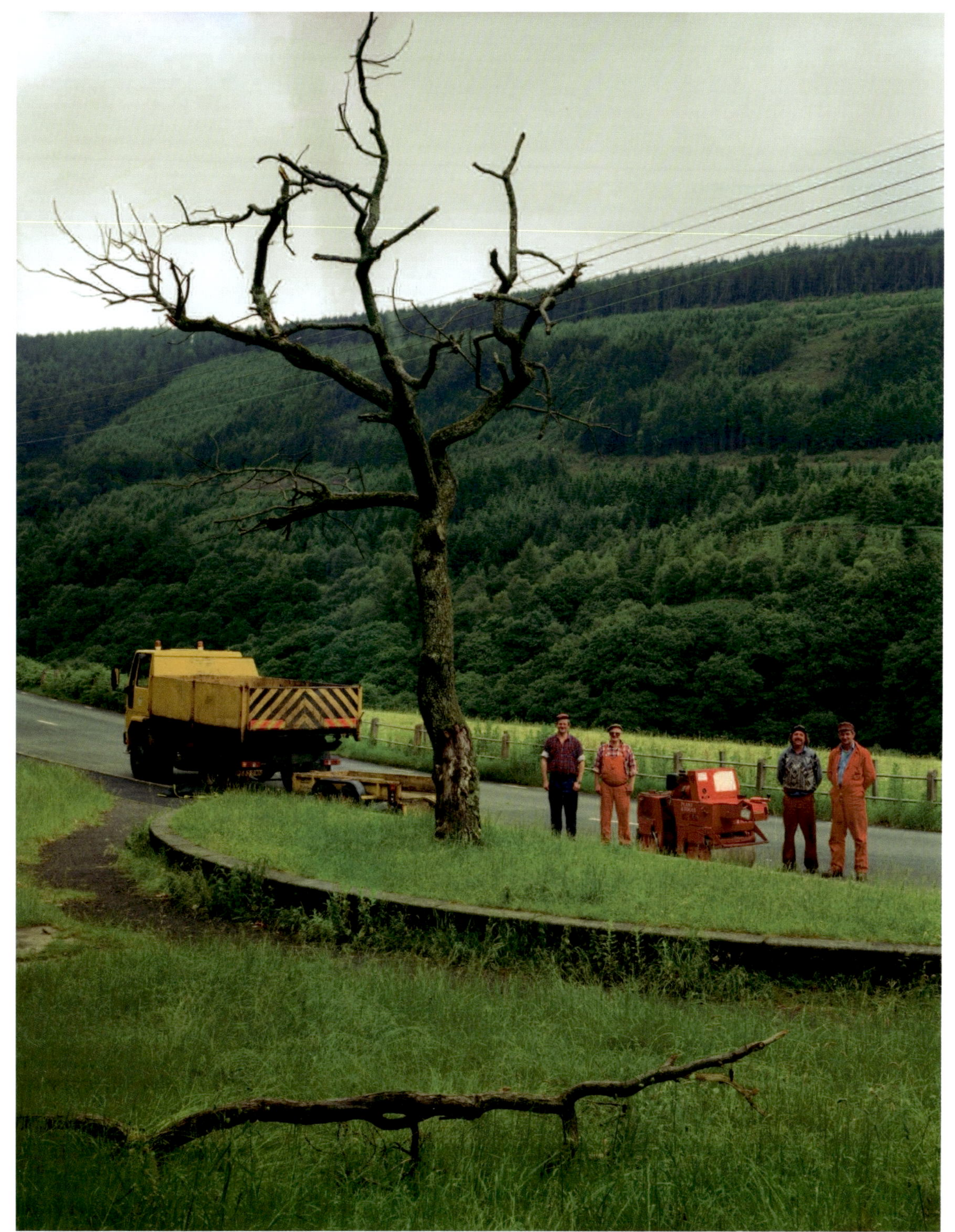

Road Workers
Duffryn

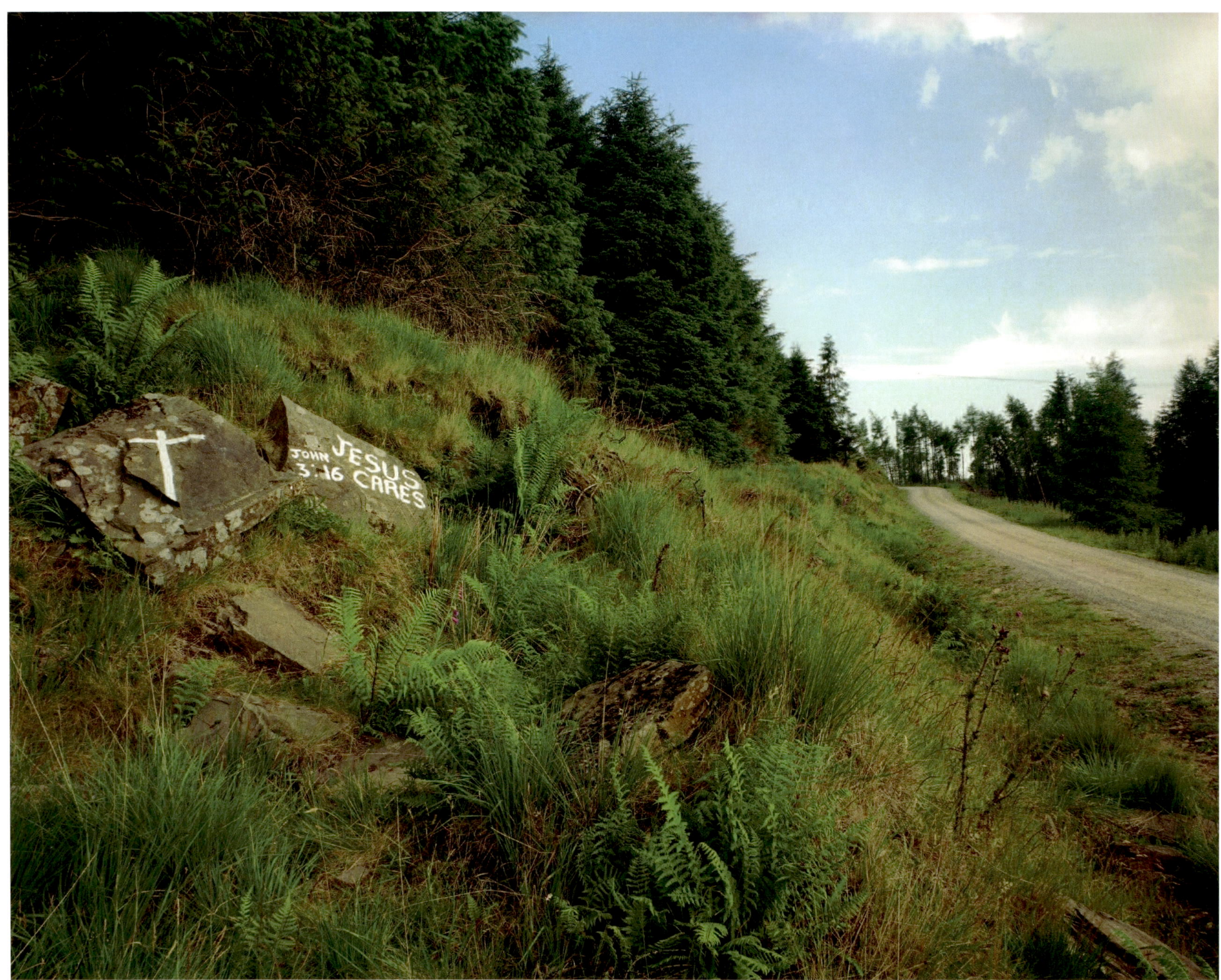

Forest Road, Croeserw

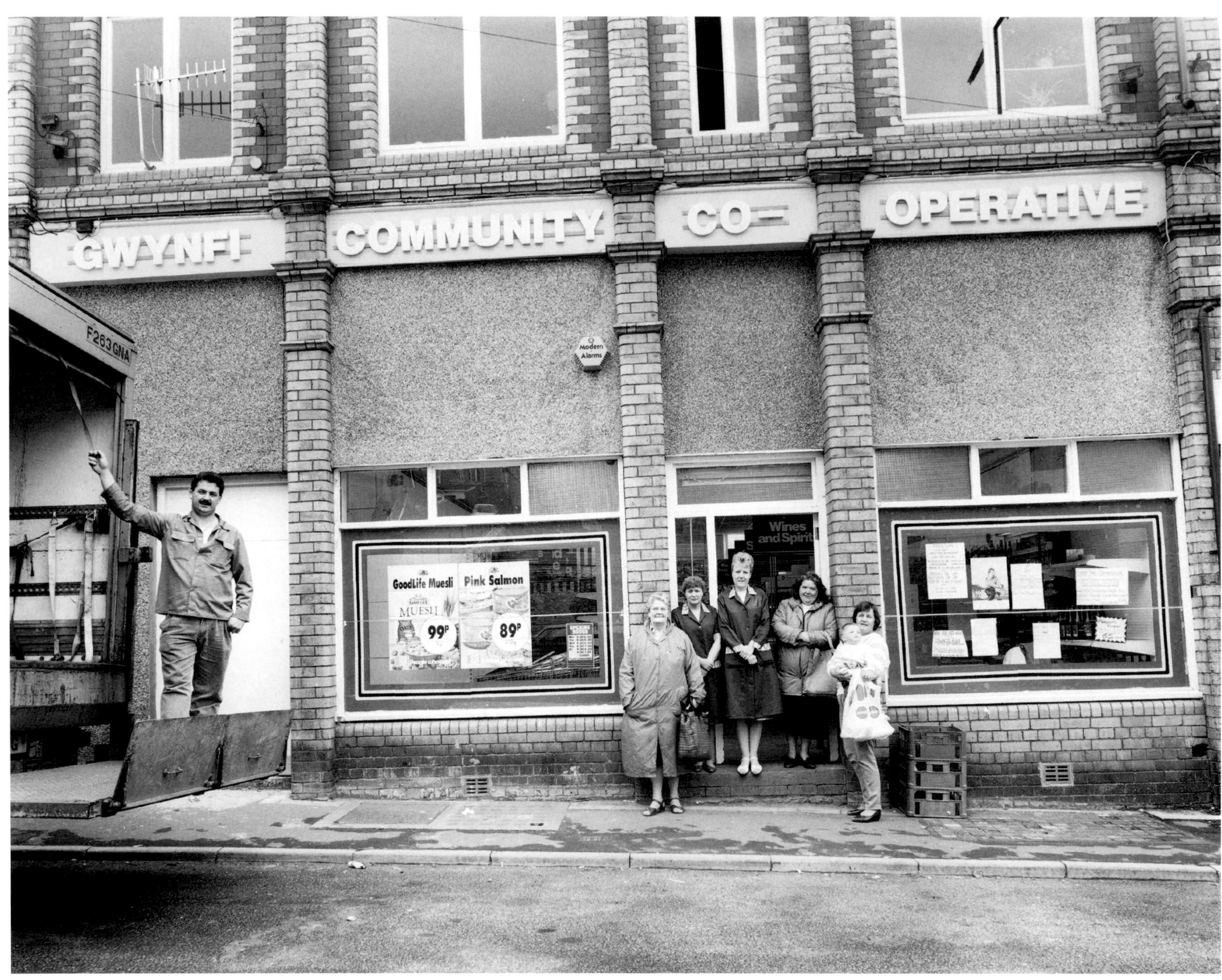

Co-op, Jersey Road, Blaengwynfi

The Project

A response (1996)

Tina Carr & Annemarie Schöne

By 1969 the last working mine in the Upper Afan Valley had closed, condemning its many small communities to dependency on the dole. The following year the Home Secretary announced in Parliament the launching of the National Community Development Project as a 'neighbourhood based experiment aimed at finding new ways of meeting the needs of people living in areas of high social deprivation'. The experiment was originally conceived and planned on a number of basic assumptions…

'…that problems of urban deprivation had their origins in the deviant pathologies of individuals and that these could best be resolved by better field co-ordination of the personal social services, combined with the mobilisation of self-help and mutual aid in the community.'

Say again? 'Problems of urban deprivation have their origins in the deviant pathologies of individuals'? That can't be right. What about the effects of unemployment, lack of resources, poverty, disempowerment, loss of identity and sense of function? Deviant individuals, if that is what they are, take the blame for a national outbreak of social and psychic disintegration? This is how the Government was thinking in 1970. It isn't difficult to identify the deviants and they are not the people living in enforced urban deprivation.

Twelve of these Community Development Project experiments were set up in small areas thought to be experiencing severe and multiple deprivation, with a team of professional workers, employed by a sponsoring local authority, to: 'Identify needs, foster community involvement and build a communication bridge between people and local services.'

The Upper Afan Valley, with its main villages of Glyncorrwg, Abergwynfi, Blaengwynfi, Cymmer and Croeserw containing in total 8,655 souls, was selected – the only Welsh example.

The project area was centred on the upper reaches of the valley, deep in the South Wales Coalfield. Ten miles north of Port Talbot, it consists of a series of small and scattered settlements ranging in size from forty to one hundred and thirty households, the majority of which grew in response to the exploitation of high quality steam coal in the valley. Now, since the destruction of the industry, these communities face severe problems of adjustment and a rapid decline in population. The 1951 population of 9,240 stabilised at 9,320 in 1961, but by 1991 it had fallen to 8,640, a net loss of some 700 people. As the natural increase during the decade 1961–71 would have been 800, the gross migration consisted of some 1,500 people moving out of the valley.

The valley experienced a rapidly declining economic base. Jobs lost in pit closures were not replaced by new alternative employment opportunities – there were 2,978 local job opportunities in 1961 compared with 245 in 1971, and worse still at the end of October 1996 there were only four jobs on offer in the Cymmer job centre. The only employment opportunities are now, as then, located along the coastal plain of South Wales, the M4 corridor and in the valley mouth towns of Bridgend, Port Talbot, Neath and Swansea. For this reason the adjustments which the local communities have been able to make in the face of rapid and considerable changes (the closure of the coal mines and the withdrawal of the previously comprehensive rail services – decisions in which local people had little voice) have been limited. Low average incomes and below normal car ownership levels have made it difficult for residents to obtain employment outside the area. Consequently unemployment rates are high, 65% in men, and a large proportion of families and individuals depend entirely on Social Security benefits.

The incredible fact is that the Community Development Project was set up with a so-called 'Action Research Strategy' to investigate all these aspects, which it did admirably, producing report after report on its findings. But as a consequence of all this hard work over five years, and based upon the findings and conclusions of all twelve CDPs, what did our enlightened Government of the day do to alleviate the problems and misery of all these multi-deprived communities? Yes,

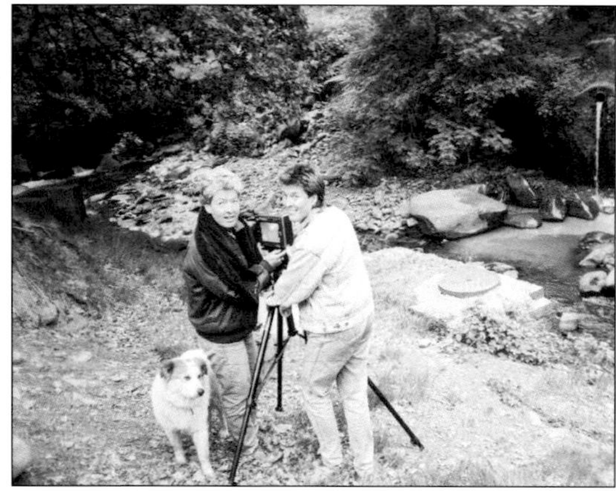

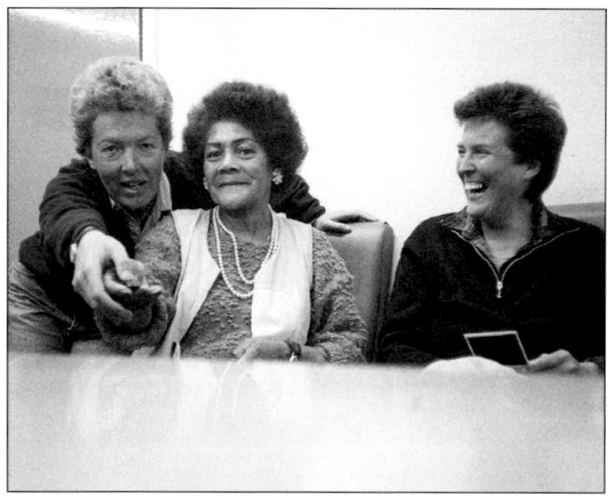

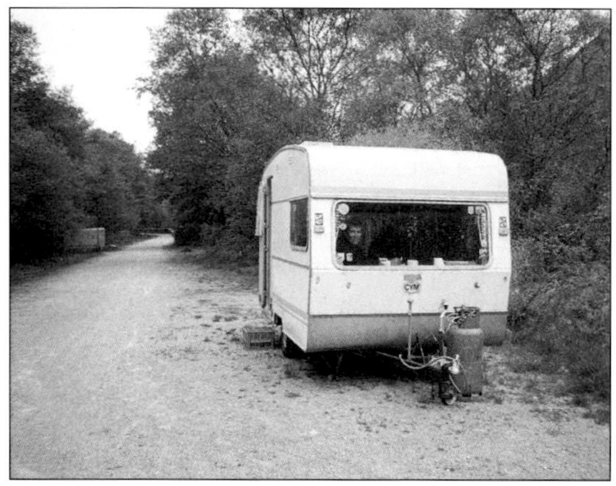

you've guessed. Absolutely nothing. The situation in Upper Afan today, thirty years later, is almost exactly as it was when the pits closed. Very little has changed. A few cosmetic exercises; the odd WDA factory unit, lying empty; some of the old housing stock upgraded externally – but remarkably little else has altered. There are still no jobs; many of the young continue to leave the valley as soon as they are able. The road infrastructure and public transport facilities are, if anything, worse than they were twenty years ago and now there is a second, and a third up and coming generation, dependent on Social Security benefits. Why? It can only be that this comparatively small number of people has become superfluous to requirements and is in fact dispensable. Not worth bothering about. That is certainly how they feel. Overlooked, forgotten, abandoned, as if they didn't exist. Well, how would anyone feel if they had been used in an experiment, a vivarium? Led to believe that help was at hand, that something would come of their participation in the CDP project – whereas nothing did.

The geography of the location plays its part too; at the head of the valley, remote, isolated, tucked away and invisible. People feel trapped, imprisoned in their environment and spiritually deprived. Whereas before, when the trains were running, they were mobile, not only for their working life but for social enrichment: trips to the seaside, Aberafan Sands, to the January sales, football, Saturday night at the pictures. You could go anywhere you liked, you were in touch, you could participate, you had the choice.

Typically the most severely deprived in material terms are also the least influential in social and political terms and the two conditions interact. These groups do not have any control over resources and they continually suffer from their inability to meet their own reasonable needs. This is what deprivation means – unmet need, a multiplicity of unmet needs. The whole population is affected detrimentally by the lack of employment, adequate income, decent housing, good health, educational opportunities, an unpolluted environment, recreational amenities and a range of goods and services which are regarded as reasonable or essential by society as a whole. Consequently the individual, group or community as a whole lacks or loses power to execute even minor decisions about personal or communal needs and resources, since decisions and policies which may alleviate or exacerbate these problems are made well away from them in the very regional or national centres responsible for the decisions that caused the problems in the first place. Seats of Government. Even the value of their combined voting power can't help them because firstly it isn't large enough and secondly most of the valley people are, by now, too apathetic to use it, realising that it can't make the slightest difference to their local situation.

Even for those whose wages and conditions are poor, the rhythm of work gives life meaning. The achievement of new tasks, the acquisition of skills and the social intercourse that is part and parcel of work experience are not something human beings want to avoid; they want and need it. Above all, work offers a sense of place in a hierarchy of social relations, both within the organisation and beyond it, and men and women are, after all, social beings. Those who work belong, those who do not are excluded.

It is difficult for people who live in the South Wales Valleys to make sense of what is happening to them in the aftermath of mining; their very reason for existing having been wiped out. They have, as in the case of Upper Afan, been denied for two generations the basic need to participate in the necessary work of society. It is impossible to exaggerate what a denial of human energies and powers this is. Insecurity, futility, lack of participation, not merely in consumption, but in active engagement in the production of useful and necessary things; the growth in crime, violence, drug abuse and the breakdown of neighbourhood and kinship networks has created a people in a kind of limbo, without identity, left to 'cope' with life and 'manage' with what they've got.

We have been working in Upper Afan periodically for the last six years. We began as Artists in Residence for a twelve-week period in 1990 funded by the Arts Council of Wales. Our workshops with the communities were challenging for many reasons. We found widespread apathy everywhere. Young people were initially disinterested, aggressive, and had very low thresholds of concentration. Senior Citizens, the most organised section of the population, were enthusiastic but preferred to be entertained rather than actively involved. Those between were the most difficult to reach. Women tied to the home raising children and men almost invisible. Many are involved in the black economy and consequently loath to come into contact with people they do not know. Many times we were taken for DSS snoopers and had great difficulty dispelling this fear.

It soon became apparent that the twelve weeks of our residency was never going to be enough. Through sheer determination and hard work, but nearing the end of our time, we began to feel that real progress was possible and that we must try to find a way to continue working with the communities who, by this time, had come to accept our being there and were beginning to participate in the projects with enthusiasm.

We, for our part, felt an obligation to be positive under difficult circumstances. We realised that our funding would end and we would leave everyone up in the air; which is what happened. We tried hard to persuade the Arts Council that more money should be found to continue (not necessarily with us) and although they agreed that it should, they felt that other agencies should contribute as they could not justify further expenditure in Upper Afan to their many other clients at a time when arts funding was already spread pretty thin.

We contacted many other agencies – Port Talbot Borough Council, the Welsh Development Agency, the Development Board for Rural Wales, British Steel, British Petroleum – in our attempts to enlist support but with negative results.

Eventually, the following year, we raised funds from the Calouste Gulbenkian Foundation for a Community Video Project in which we proposed to make a film describing life in the valley through the eyes of its residents.

Having established a need for self-expression in the community we decided that the making of the video was the next vital step in stimulating further activity. We felt that the video would give people a great, immediate sense of self-esteem and purpose to be able to express their own opinions, wants and needs for themselves, in a medium that is familiar to them, albeit via soap operas and American wrestling.

The video project was very successful. A wide variety of people from the very young to the very old were encouraged to talk to camera, to express their views on what they thought should or should not happen in their valley. The most common complaint was that things were done over their heads; without consultation. In other words, they were not asked what they thought should be done, and if they were, by chance, then their suggestions were overlooked, overruled.

The residents of Upper Afan may feel isolated and alone but the sad fact is that they are not. Their problems, their needs, their aspirations are shared by many millions of people around the globe to greater or lesser extents. They are for us a microcosm representing many of the failures of our systems – economic, political, human – to address the issues blanketly called progress. Scientific and technological advances are reducing people to anonymous numbers. Depriving people of meaningful work is only part of a very complex equation pertaining to man's inability to keep in proportion his uses of the technology he has created in relation to the quality of life lived by the majority of people on earth.

TC & AS, 1996

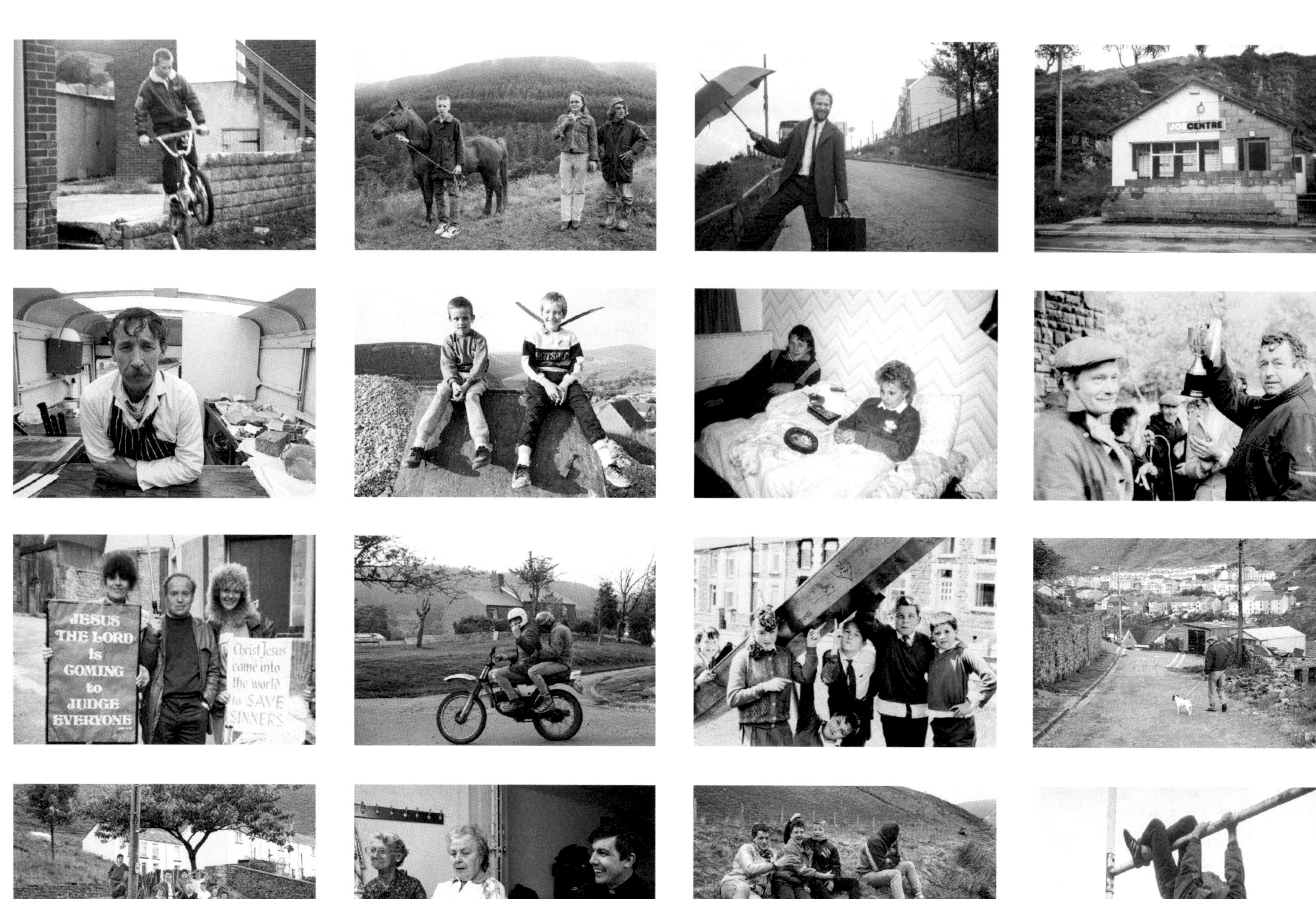

Photographs made by the community in workshops with the 'Artists in Residence' (April – June 1990)

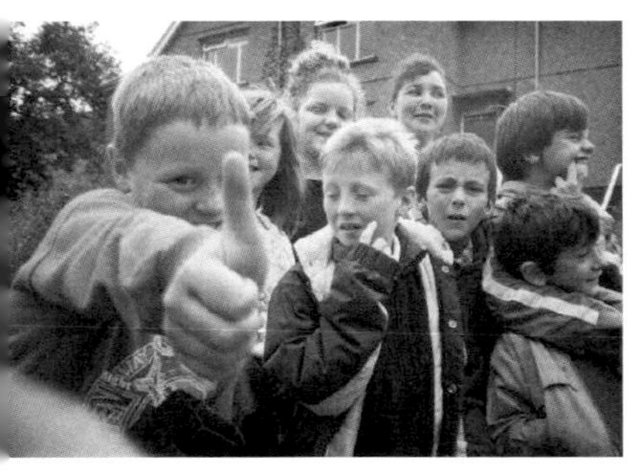
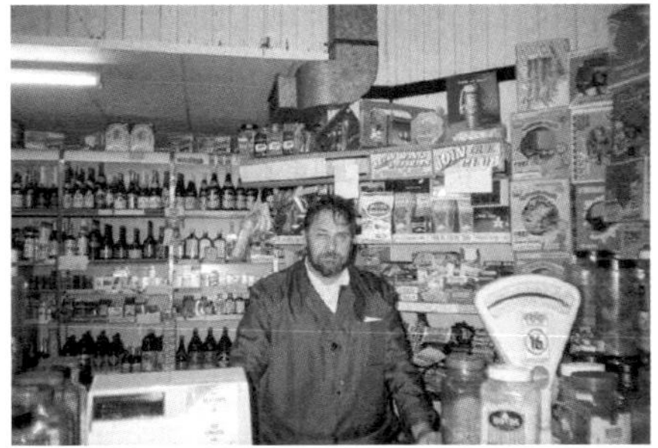
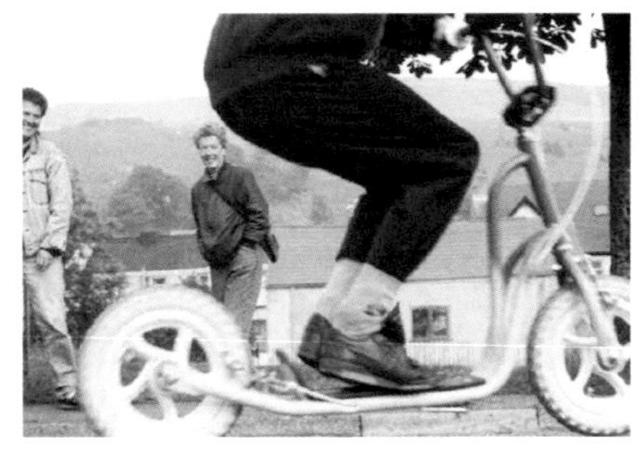
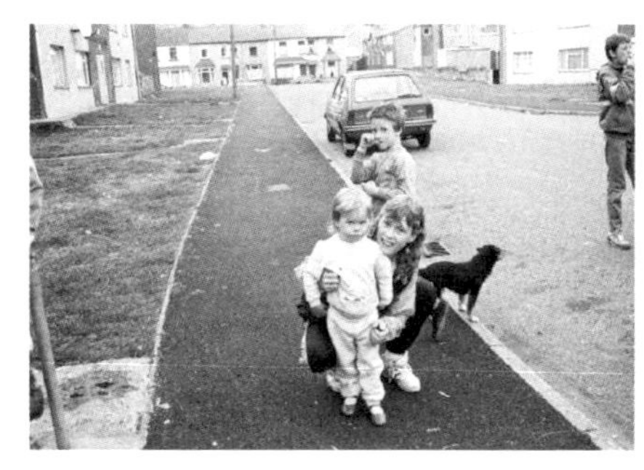
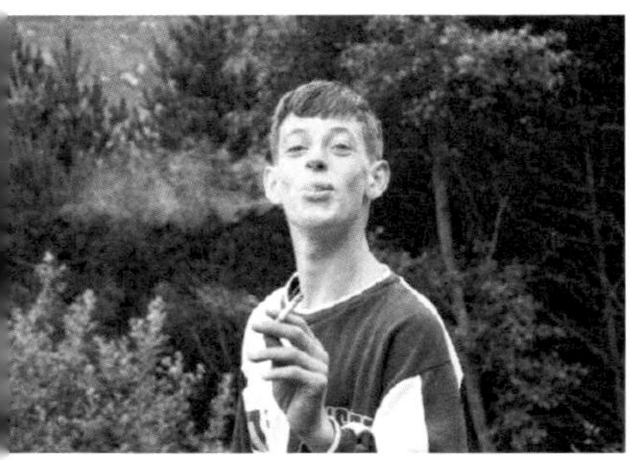
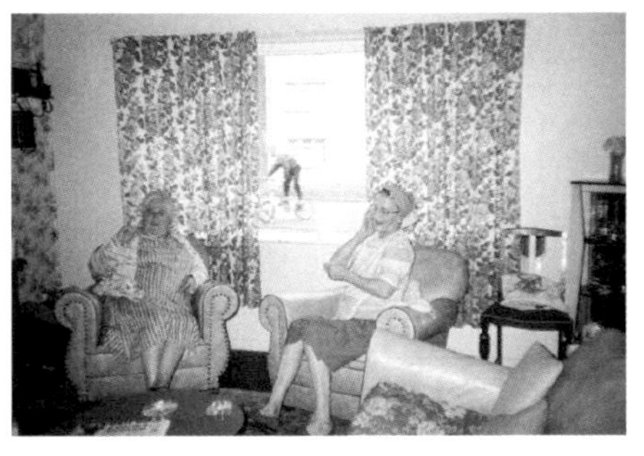
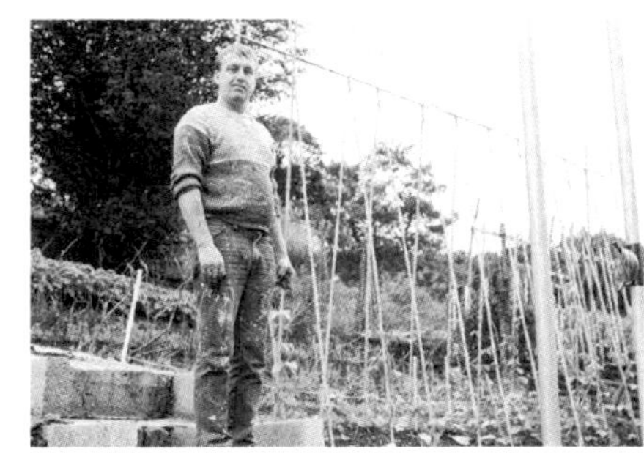
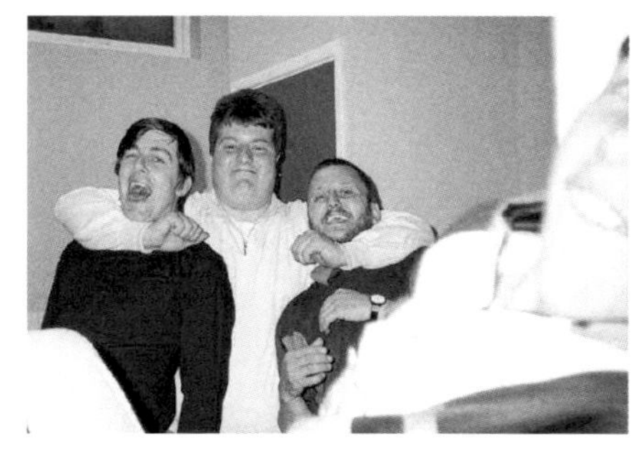
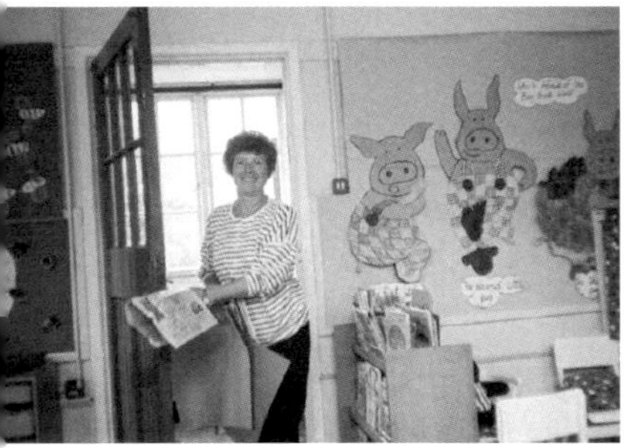
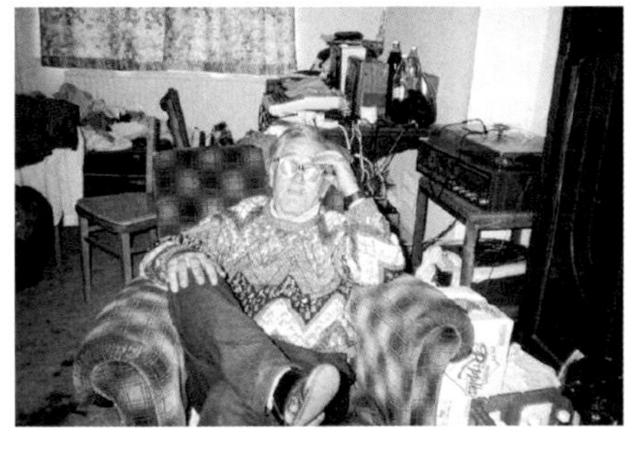
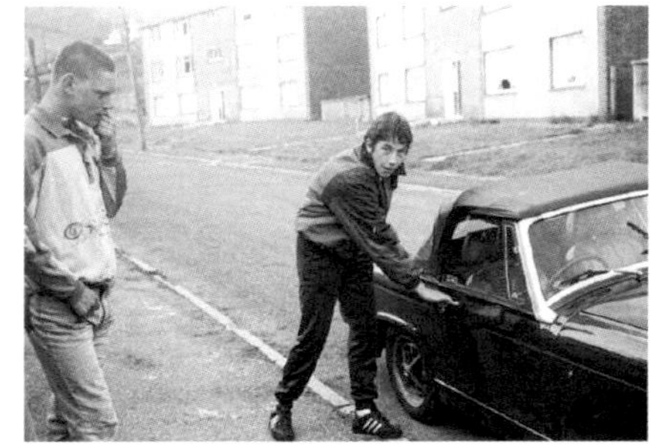
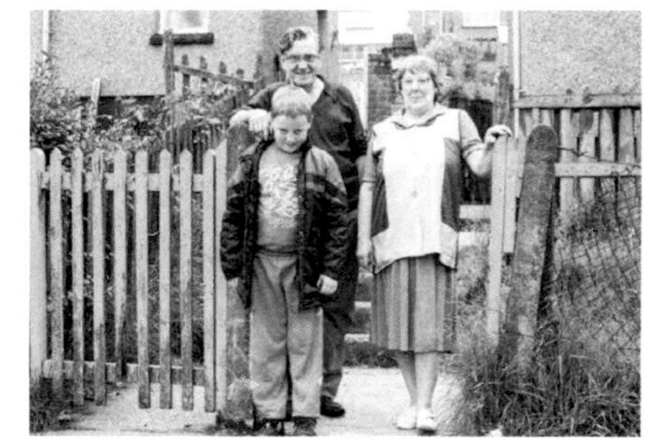
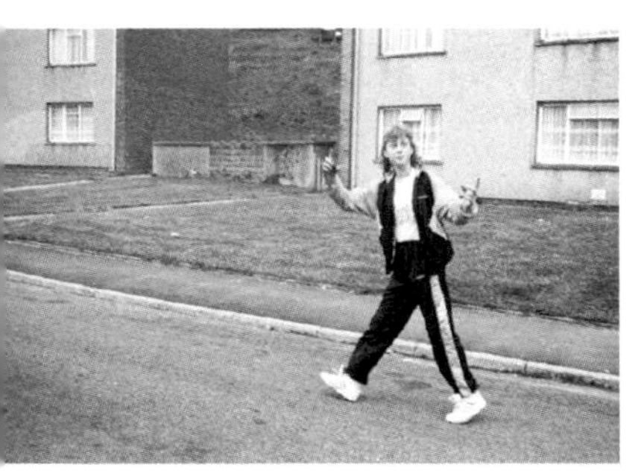
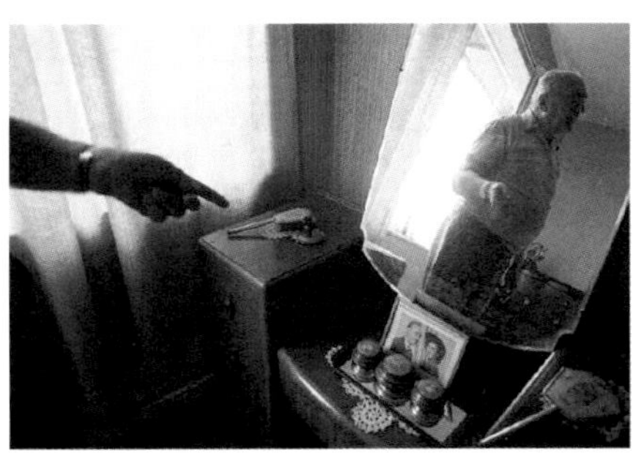
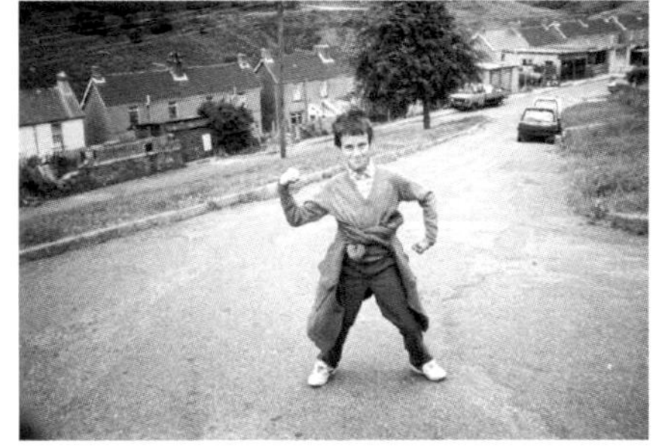
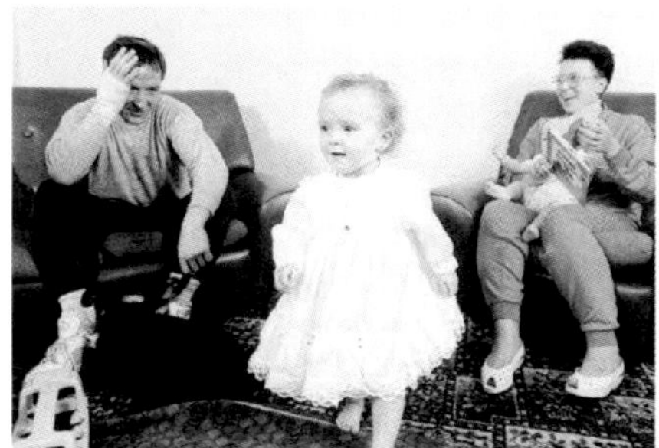

Interviews

with Valley Residents

Bert Ackery

A miner all his working life (1934–1967) at South Pit, Glyncorrwg and Dyffryn Rhondda Colliery

The age of fourteen we all left school then, unless you were fortunate and went on to grammar school education, but you would have to have money in those days to do that. So most of us left at fourteen and there was nothing else for us except to go down the pit – South Pit. I was a fortnight over fourteen years of age – the smallest boy in the pit at the time. On the photograph [taken to mark his first day as a miner] you can see the water carrier, the 'jacks' as we used to call them – when I was carrying that I was so small that it was rubbing on the floor. I used to carry the lamps as well. Six days a week it was then, 1934. Hard work it was – up at 5.30am. My father was working there as well so I used to go out with him in the morning, call for one or two people on the way and we'd all walk up together. Down by 7.00am, up at 3.00pm. We'd go down the shaft and then walk to our place of work – there was no transport down there then.

My first job was 'collier boy'. I filled trams with coal; working with another man who cut the coal and I filled it into the trams – hard work for a little boy. I would have liked to do something else, no doubt, but I had no choice. I became a deputy in charge of a particular part of the mine, safety especially. It was my job to see that everything was right for the people working there. Underground, you had gas – methane gas – and you had to see that the ventilation was right so that if anything happened to the ventilation, it had to be put right or you had to take the men from there. We had an explosion, fortunately not on my shift. Twenty-one were badly burned, but it could have been much worse – the whole pit could have gone up.

I moved to Dyffryn Rhondda as training officer. All the new boys came through me and I would see that they were trained properly. Any men that came in, going on to other jobs, came under me. I co-ordinated all the training. I also lectured in first aid. I started with the St John's Ambulance Brigade when I was eleven years of age. Every colliery had ambulance men appointed. We used to get £5 a year on top of our wages for 'carrying the box' – a first aid box it was; and anything that happened in the colliery then we had to go and see to it. There were a lot of accidents at that time, broken arms, legs – we had to organise all the procedures for getting them out. As you can understand, it was such a long way underground – you couldn't get a doctor to them – not quickly – it could take two hours or more. Later on, we were allowed to give morphia. We were the only persons in the country, not medically trained, who were allowed to give morphia.

When I started, in 1934, my wages were 13s 2d a week, for over forty hours. I progressed from collier boy to working with the horses. At one time there was over eighty horses in the colliery. They were all stabled underground. If they were fortunate, they could come up once a year. Hostlers looked after them, fed them, cleaned them out. Some of the horses were treated better than the men actually. I don't know where the expression 'pit ponies' came from, because they weren't ponies, they were fully grown horses.

I loved my horses. They were good horses and, if you treated a horse well, it would look after you too. One saved my life as a matter of fact. My brother and I were working together and we had the horse there. We sat down to have our food and I said to my brother, 'What's the matter with him then?' – very restless he was – 'Quack' was the name of the horse – 'What's the matter with him, very restless, aye, we'd better go from here,' I said. So with that the whole place caved in. Our food and everything was left behind, my brother's clothes – the horse sensed it. Horses sensed a lot underground – wonderful animals. The people who were driving horses came to depend on them, not just for the work, but for their own safety. Marvellous animals. I loved my horses.

Then I went onto machines – a 'joy loader' – it worked on caterpillar tracks. It had a scoop on the front that gathered up the coal and then it was conveyed behind you. I think I broke the record on that one – I moved one hundred and twenty tons in one shift.

How did you meet your wife?
We were both born in the village. We were courting for six years before we got married. We used to go to the local cinema in the Workman's Hall – pretty derelict now. It was built in 1924 from the miners' subscriptions – 3d a week. It was built out of the efforts of the local workmen – it was a lovely place, a great place. It had billiard rooms, card rooms, reading rooms upstairs, library, cinema, ballroom, newspapers – people would be in there every morning to read the newspapers. My uncle was the caretaker. I was the relief caretaker, if he wasn't well or anything. We had our own generator – I used to start her up, great big flywheels she had – it wasn't on the mains. My uncle lived in Bridge Street and my wife lived next door to him. She was the cleaner at the hall – she went in every morning – the place was spotless.

There were 'pictures' every night of the week and on Saturday there were two houses. We had all the good films. The 'cowboys' were my favourites. We had a lot for our money – it wasn't just the big picture – we had the news, a supporting picture, then perhaps a cartoon and then the big picture. Films changed twice a week, organised by the secretary – the best seats were only a shilling and sixpence the others – we got our money's worth. We had dances downstairs in the ballroom – we had our own bands, quite a few local bands came and played the old dance music – it was great.

You are on the Workman's Hall Committee. Were there any plans to revitalise it?
It is so difficult with the Hall now. No-one wants to go there, the state it's in. The rugby club is there now keeping it warm – if it wasn't for them it would deteriorate even more, fall down probably. But they'll be going from there soon. They've got a plot of land to build their own club – can't blame them really – they want their own place.

I had an idea for the Hall, I thought that, if we could attract some investment, we could have put a swimming pool in the hall where the ballroom was – where the rugby club is now. Something for the youngsters. The ground slopes there and it's all solid rock. There's a cavity underneath it which could be excavated out to make a pool. The trouble is you got to have money to do it. The Coal Board should have been committed to doing these kinds of things at least. The coal owners and the Coal Board made their money in the collieries and now they've gone – just gone from here and left the place desolate. They didn't put anything back in here, nothing – they took everything from here and left us with nothing. Just the building – which is our building. The Coal Board had nothing to do with the building but surely they could give us something in return for what they've had from the village?

The local authorities, well I suppose their hands are tied with the amount of money available to them in this particular climate. As it is now, everyone is crying for money. I think the Coal Board should have been made to look after these little villages. We are not the only ones – it's right through the whole of South Wales. They just

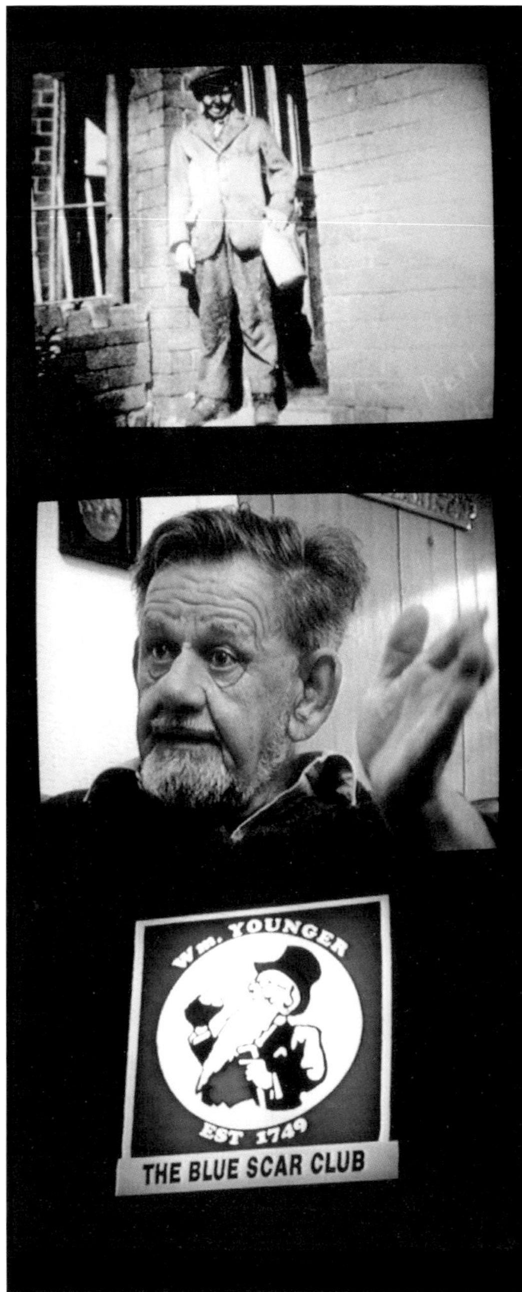

plundered the coal from here, shut down the collieries and it's bye-bye and they're gone.

After the pit closed, we formed a committee in the village, to see what could be done with the old colliery buildings, the ones they didn't bulldoze. They said they would leave the pithead gear there and the double decker, pithead baths, they said, could be made into a museum. On top of that, we thought, we could have a narrow-gauge railway coming up from Cymmer. We even had the engine down at Cymmer waiting to be put into operation – stored in the old fire-station, it was. In my opinion it would have been a real money-spinner, but nobody would give us the money. The Welsh Office didn't want to know us and we were not in Europe then. Everything fell through and they put the museum down at Dyffryn – Afan Argoed, nice country setting, but not a colliery. A colliery museum is a colliery and the colliery is here. And another thing we have here is the old miners' cottages. The deeds of this house go back to 1820 but I have it on good authority that the house is much older, probably dating back to 1750. We could have done one of these old cottages out like at St Fagans, that and the narrow-gauge railway – it would employ people and bring tourists. There's nothing stopping them doing it now – the Ponds Project – they could do it. Everything has just gone downhill now.

After thirty-three years down the mine I've got the legacy of being underground – a bad chest. Everyone who has been underground has a bad chest. But we don't qualify for compensation, because we haven't got enough dust. Everybody has dust. My father was fifty-six years underground and they said he never had any dust. Emphysema, bronchitis – they won't admit that we've got dust – but we keep on having coughs and colds the whole year through. Fog is terrible weather for us. There was no thought of using masks then, or earmuffs. They do now; but in our day we didn't have any of those things. It was hard, hard work – and now there's nothing at all. When they closed the colliery they closed the village. There's a bit of work to be had outside the valley, I suppose. The steel works, but that involves travelling and firms these days want their workforce on the doorstep. It's terrible for these youngsters today. A lot of revolutionary thinking needs to be done to get work back to the people. I don't know the answer to it – I don't know.

Mark & Alan

Organisers of a gym in the
derelict Miners' Hall, Glyncorrwg

Mark: I started training here in 1980 with another man who set this place up. He moved away and took most of his stuff but he 'tributed what weights and gear he didn't need like and I took it over. The Hall was there for us already – been going downhill like since the mines closed – was it '63 or '64, something like that. Nobody cared about it – kids vandalised it.

Everyone else have had their halls done up like. If it wasn't for the rugby club this place would have fallen down b'now. When it's sold – it has been sold like – so we hear – when it's closed we'll have nowhere else to go. We tried for the Old Ambulance Hall but the 'Ponds' have had that, beat us to it like. We need a permanent place, a proper place. You can't hump weights around, benches – they're heavy like – and we need to put things up the walls.

There's about twenty of us, ten little ones, the rest our age. At the moment we are just paying the rugby club for the electric – a tribute like – and we charge the boys twenty pence a night. That's the only way we can do it – not a lot like – just covers the electric.

I got laid off a couple of months ago – it's well, better really – I can train more! Alan here is a welder, he got laid off a fortnight ago so now we can make a lot of our own equipment. Normally, of a Friday night, eight or nine of us come up here to train. We play our music – some do weights, then we've got the bags, skipping.... It's something to do in the nights – stops us drinking – everybody's drinking, hanging round the square – nothing else to do. We keep fit, we're healthier and we do other sports too – football, tai-kwon-do. Alan travels twenty-two miles, one way, to Swansea to do tai-kwon-do. Whatever you do you got to travel – and he goes to Swansea twice a week to college (HNC Engineering). That's another eighty miles – on £33 a week? It's all money like, to Swansea back three times a week.

We need a sports complex up here. I think the 'Ponds' is a waste of time myself. I don't think it's going to do anything for the youngsters up here. The only benefit I can see is the bailiff's fines for the kids pinching the fish. They'll be down there every night. What benefit is that for us? A sports complex in one of those factories would be ideal. Nobody is going to use those factories now – they are too far from the motorway – it's all 'A' roads. People want to go straight on, straight off the motorway these days.

Everybody else have had their workman's halls done up and made into sports complexes, like in Blaengwynfi. They shoved a shoebox on the line up here for us, with nothing in it. The first thing they gave us was badminton nets and rackets – well you can't hit the shuttlecock two feet and it's hitting the ceiling. And, the thing is, it's so small you can only do one or two things in there. Table tennis and that's about it. They put one down in Baglan, it's a thousand times better. There's a wooden floor down there, whereas ours is just tarmac; buffet bar, tabletennis tables, everything like. They shoved that shoe box down there for us as if to say 'shove that up the valleys, shove that up there'. We need a tidy gym up here; sauna, jacuzzi – where women can train as well as men. The women in the village want to keep fit too but they are on their own like. They are trying – cycling, and doing things but there's no incentive. How can you ask a woman to come and train in here? It's too rough and it's cold.

We keep fit and enjoy it. At school right, I was awful small. All I wanted was to be bigger so I started doing weights. Now I'm right. I was bigger mind, heavier – heavier weight than I am now – out here I was – but it was too much. Now I'm right. I don't like the tablet side of it like – it's

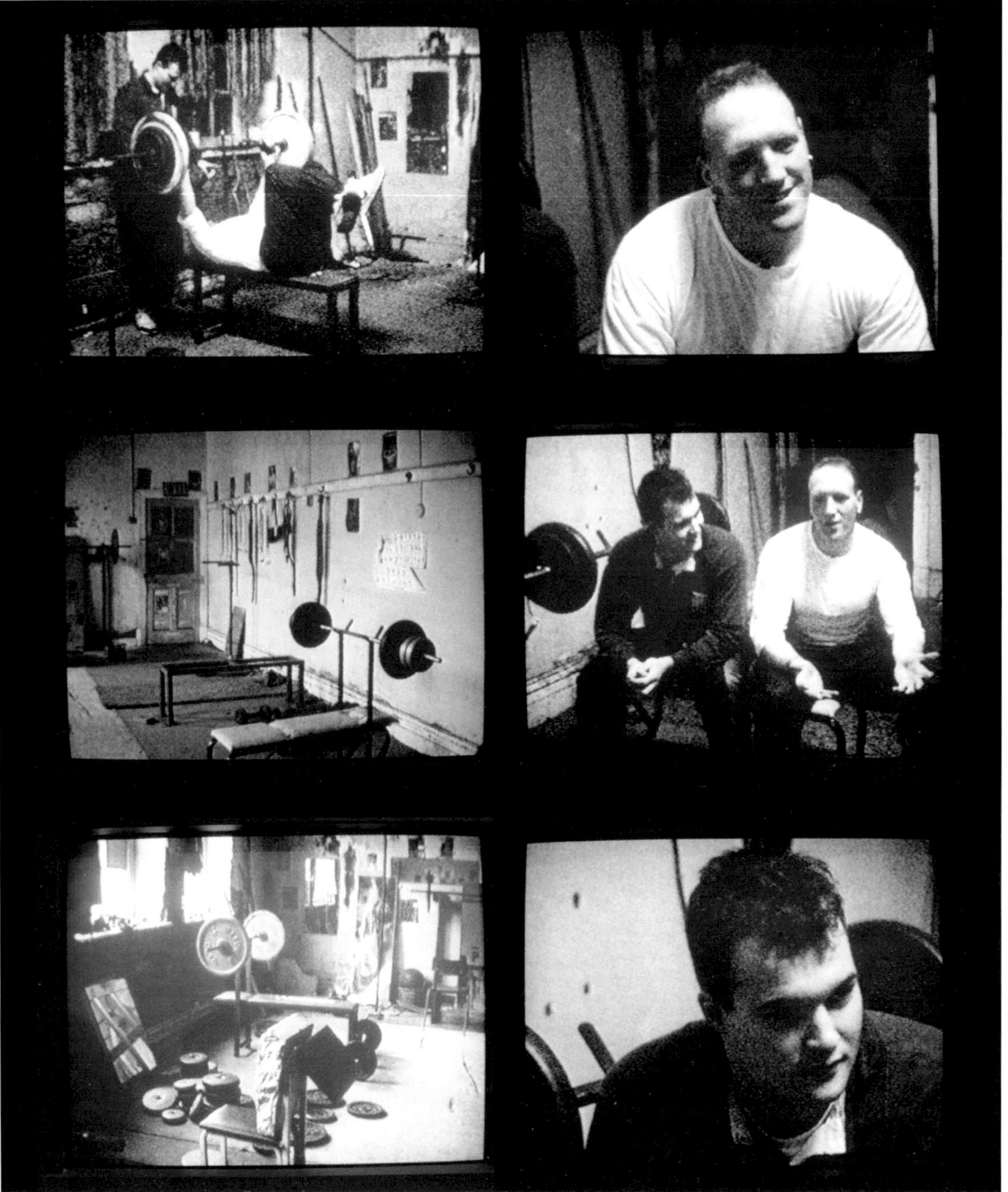

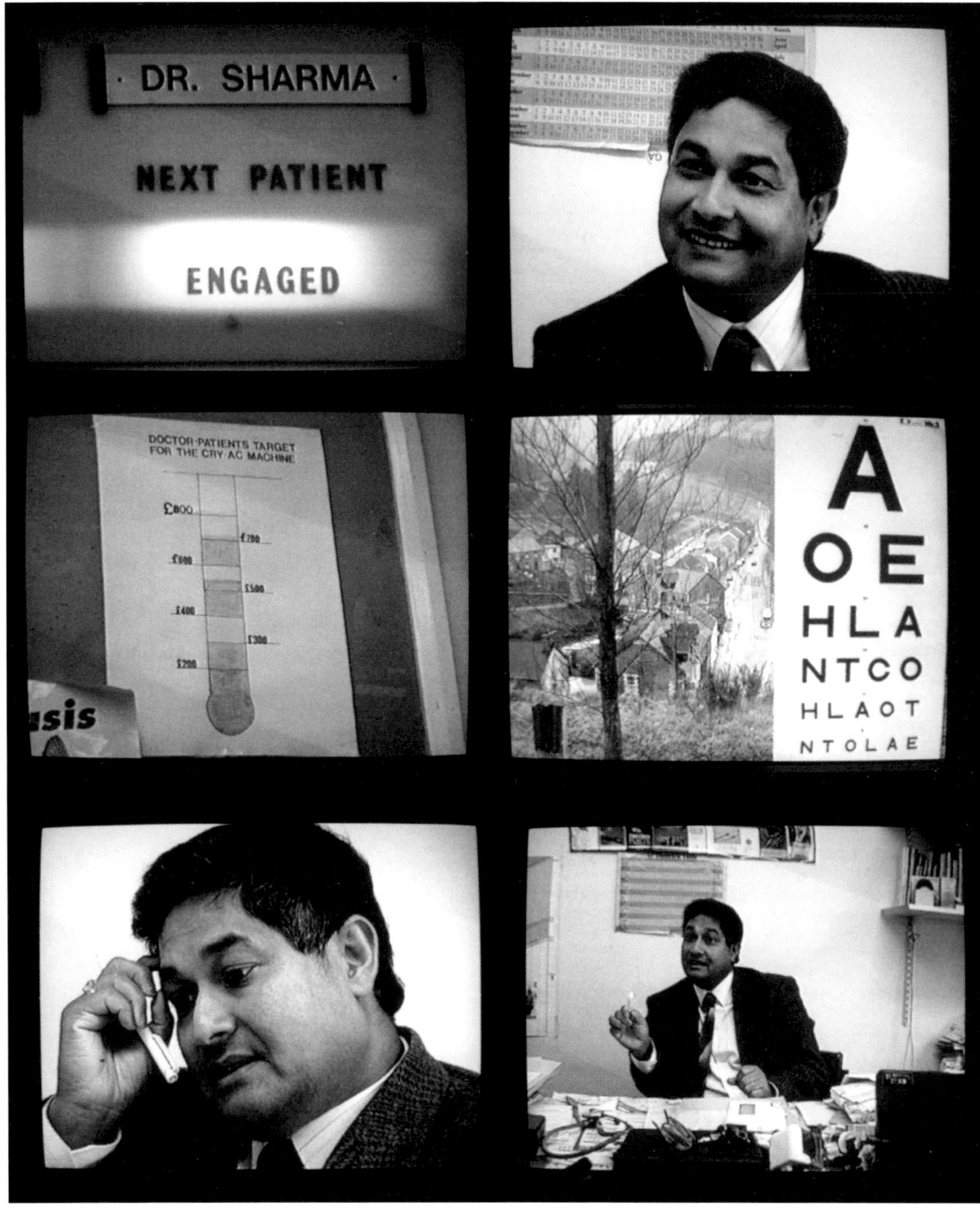

giving it a bad name. It's not so bad, vitamin C and things like that – energy tablets, but I think raw eggs can do the same job – well, they done it for me like. I got one weakness though – biscuits – I love biscuits. I eat a good diet but I got a weakness – biscuits. Alan's weakness is cider, cider and Chineses, big piles of rice – good for you!

What are your hopes, dreams for the future?

A good sports complex, made out of one of the empty factories down there. I think it could be done.

What do you think is the future for the valley?

To be honest with you, the way it's going now – ghost town – I see. I wouldn't buy a house up here anyway, there's nothing up here, nothing to do, nowhere to go.

Some people would like to train but they don't want to come in here – can't blame them really. But I like it here mind. I like to train in here – it's the feeling – the Bronx like – the atmosphere – you feel awkward in a clean gym. I've trained in Neath but it's awful strange. I want to come back home like, to the rough and rugged things – I've done it for so long – it's in the bones like – the rough and rugged old things – and that's it like. Can't just leave it like – appreciate it like.

They blame the children in the village for vandalising everything that they put up here but they never really give us anything to try and stop the kids. A lot of youngsters come on to me, 'Why don't you start a class up here for kids?' You can't start youngsters up here man – somebody fall? You could never get insurance for something like this. Discipline and they are right – but the place isn't big enough for many more. If you are hanging around waiting for weights you get cold. Then you have to warm up again. Some nights in here the bars are so cold you stick to them!

Have you seen our curtains? This used to be the Miners' Library wasn't it? These have been here since the Hall opened in 1925.

Doctor Sharma

Cymmer Health Centre

How long have you been here?

Eight years. I deal with all the day to day problems, and from the patients I can get all the information what is going on in the society.

How would you describe the general health of people here?

I would say that it is not good at all because of the various factors. People are economically and socially deprived. There are no recreational facilities available so the incidence of smoking and drinking is more. Then, all other diseases are more common here which is related to their economic and social deprivation.

Do you think unemployment has something to do with it?

Yes, unemployment means anxiety, boredom, stress factors, depression – the whole spectrum.

What are the main health problems, diseases you have to deal with?

As I said, the whole spectrum. Pneumoconiosis, asthma, diabetes, alcoholic, stress factors, anxieties. There is nothing to do, no hope. The younger generation are not doing anything so naturally they feel bored and what to do?

Are you treating the end results?

Treatment does not just mean giving medication because it's all inter-related – the mental and physical well being. If somebody is depressed – why depression? So you have to find it out – the reason. You have to sort out that reason rather than giving an anti-depressant drug. If you remove all the factors, economic, get work, recreational facilities there should be no reason at all.

You've been burgled recently, was it for drugs? Is there a drug problem here?

Oh yes, yes. There's a drug problem everywhere in South Wales, everywhere. And we have no burglar alarm. You can't fight for everything so I have to say let it be broken – it's not my property anyway.

Do you ever feel as if you can't cope with it sometimes?

I have to cope but I think the government and the media could do more to help people understand their situation. Mass education through the media, these are the only factors that can improve the situation. Say, for example, immunisation. Immunisation is not very high here although our practice staff, the Health Visitor, District Nurse try their best to get people into the surgery. A lot of people still – they won't turn in. The media could do more to promote the importance of immunisation so that people are encouraged to come in. When we visit patients at home we always give leaflets but it doesn't work. Papers, leaflets – we have distributed so many. It doesn't work. The waiting room is full of leaflets – nobody wants to know. I don't think it's good communication.

Television, video?

If they see anything on television, adverts for drugs, they come the next morning and say, 'I want it.' Because of the television. Any new drug on *Tomorrow's World* – the next morning they say, 'Can I have it?' Simple thing. Without knowing any of the details, side effects or what; it doesn't matter. I would like to see more mass education programmes so that people will know themselves and know what to do. It is necessary for the development of all societies. More beneficial than treating the patient by giving the drugs.

Do you need more funds?

That is the main thing. Then we could send out more people into the community, dieticians, physiotherapists. The most essential thing is the preventative side. More important than the curative. In fact, you are not solving the problem without doing the preventative work.

Carol

Senior member of the management team with responsibility for sales – UK Extrusion & Plastic Bags Ltd

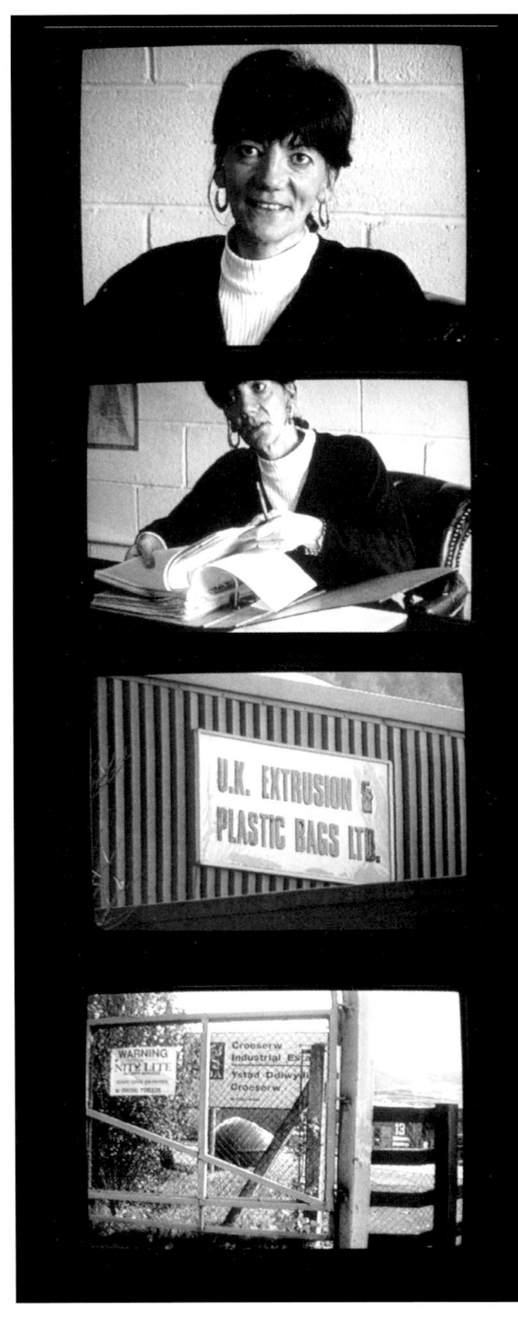

We only produce a small amount of plastic bags now but we import them from Europe and the Far East. We supply some of the biggest chain stores in the country – supermarkets, but unfortunately we don't produce much here now. Two years ago we had a fire – up until then we were producing a lot in this factory. At the time of the fire we had seventy-five people working here; now there's only twelve.

Is the industrial estate here in Croeserw full?

No, there is only one other company here apart from us. Since I've been here, that's six years, there has been only one or two small workshops set up then gone again. The WDA do their best. I mean people look at us and think what are you doing here, but it's got a great deal to offer and I think if they realised that – but there's other places they prefer to go.

How do you find the workforce?

Great – no problem. We wouldn't have been able to carry on the last few years without their co-operation. Nobody minds what they do – if it has to be done then somebody will do it – and that I find is great. I'm from London and used to places where there is a lot of employment – there isn't any more – but there's not so much one job one person in this company – the people we've got now are fantastic. You always get the odd one mind you, but I find as long as people are treated fairly….

Do you get a lot of applications for jobs?

About two a month. I've got nothing to offer at the moment but every letter is answered. We get mostly enquiries for unskilled, general labouring and from outside the valley for sales because, of course, it doesn't matter where you live for sales. We don't have a high turnover here – most of our people have been here as long as I have – six or seven years. We have one YTS boy who's been with us a year but apart from that…. We don't get applications from youngsters, school-leavers because they can't work the night shift; factory work doesn't appeal and from the ones I've spoken to it seems, well it seems as if they've given up. I mean, they are told there is not work up here – it's easy to give up. As I say, it's easy for me to say – I'm sitting here with a job.

Have you got orders?

Yes we have. We are in a better position than a lot of people and of course, we could do with a few more customers but nobody's buying, and if people are not buying, then nobody is using plastic bags. And now it seems that people are cutting down on food, not buying so much food – so they are not wanting bags for that either.

How do you see the future of the valley?

I don't know. I get very upset. It's difficult to say. People will invest in places like Bridgend – the bigger companies – but people are not willing to come here and give it a try. I am sure if they did they'd learn by it. Manufacturers, like us, prepared to train – the workforce is here – I can't speak highly enough of them. Sometimes they were asked to do things that were not part of their job and always they did it – and did it well.

Have you had problems with vandalism?
Yes, from the kids on the estate. The youngsters built a camp in the factory. I mean – if one of them had lit a cigarette or something, the whole place would have gone up. Plastics! Not only that, the stuff is in bales – it could have fallen on them. And chemicals – not here – but other places – the kids just don't realise the danger it is to them.

Vandalism with the older youths is a problem. With the little ones it isn't intended – they just want a bit of fun. It has gone down a bit lately but it's a community problem – people must be aware – it's not just here – it's everywhere. At one time we had lorries outside which we used to load up overnight. We had to stop it because there was too much damage to them. You would come in in the morning and they were completely wrecked – that damages business. There is a night guard now but these kinds of things don't encourage firms to come to the area. People must be aware that they can stop it. Somebody is doing it and somebody knows that it is being done. It's the ones eight to fourteen that worry me and that is because of the danger – the older ones – well, they should know better.

What are your hopes and fears?
If we ride the recession we will be OK. But as far as the valley is concerned, I don't know. The demise of Maesteg over the valley wasn't so much because of the pits closing down but because Revlon, the biggest employer, stopped taking on part-time ladies. Theirs was the second wage. That hit very hard – but now, I hear, they've started employing again and they're doing very well, so maybe some people from this valley can filter down to Maesteg. So there's a bit of hope there.

I think people have got to realise that if they want a job they have to travel. And by travelling I don't mean great distances – I mean to Bridgend, Port Talbot – out of the valley. Fares are a problem. If their fares are £10 a week and the wages are quite low then the best thing to do is organise lifts or buses – that's the way. But people must be prepared to travel. There is a little bit of work if people want it but they have got to travel – the work isn't going to come to them, not up the valley.

It's easier once you are in work, and that's the dreadful thing, it's a known fact that once you are in work it's easier to find work. My advice would be to take anything – anything that's going – because that is experience. It's experience to actually get up in the morning and go to work. Attendance is very important. It's more of a problem for women I think. Women are under a great deal of pressure when they work – they are under far more pressure than men. Children, running the house, and they really do need a co-operative partner otherwise it's almost impossible. It annoys me when people say women only work for pin money. They are very lucky if they do – and they are in a nice job. But people don't come to factories to work if they don't need the money – it's not easy – the jobs are not nice.

People say to us – 'How can you run a factory up here?' – but we've had no problem at all with transport or anything. People say, 'You're cut off in the winter' – but touch wood, we've never been cut off as long as I've been here. Our lorries come over Maesteg. We get them to come off the motorway at Junction 36 because it is difficult with the big lorries – rather than come through Port Talbot. From that point of view Croeserw is better off than say, Glyncorrwg. It is daunting, I suppose, for someone new coming in – they think we are miles from nowhere – isolated – but if they can get over that feeling they'll be well pleased.

I'm mortally offended by some of the things people say about us – as if we are in cowboy country or something – and this an attitude from people only twenty miles down the road, Bridgend, Swansea. And if people living there take that attitude what can you expect from anybody else? I mean I feel offended. Then you've got the other side of the coin where the people living here go on the defensive, perhaps it's not meant, but I can understand their point of view. What they have to realise is that they can go to Bridgend and work and be as good as anybody else – they shouldn't be put off by other people's attitudes.

Blaengwynfi Kids

Natalie, Jamie, Rhian, Lianne, Dawn & Sian

Natalie: My name is Natalie and I'm twelve.
Jamie: My name is Jamie and I'm twelve.
Rhian: I'm Rhian and I'm eleven years of age.
Lianne: Don't film me – I don't like it. My name is Lianne and I'm age twelve.

Dawn: I can't look at the camera – I can look at you though – OK? My name is Dawn and I'm fourteen.
Lianne: Right, I've got to go and meet someone. *LAUGHS.*
Sian: Who am I? Oh yes, I'm Sian and I'm eleven.

Right, question number one. Are you courting?
Natalie: Yes. No. I'm just seeing someone.

Since when?
Natalie: Tuesday.

So this is recent?
Dawn: She's just going with him.

Have you been going out somewhere?
Natalie: To the youth club in Cymmer.
Sian: And behind the garages.
Dawn: And down the bus stop.

So you meet in various places?
Natalie: We went cycling tonight but he went in 'cause he had to go to bed. I didn't go with him. LAUGHS.

Dawn, are you seeing anyone?
Dawn: Yes in Croeserw. Best friends we are.

Did you meet in school?
Dawn: No in youth club I did. He asked Natalie would I go out with him.
Natalie: He asked me to ask her.

He's shy?
Dawn: Yes, nobody asks each other up here.
No?
Dawn: The boys are poofs up here.

Are the boys shy?
Dawn: Yes, very.
Natalie: I would ask a boy though. Oh, excuse me, would you like to go out with me? LAUGHS

OK. Now let's get on a bit more. Are you all going to Cymmer Comprehensive?
Dawn: I've nearly finished. I've only got one year to go.
Jamie: Somebody came to school yesterday with a big gun see. A gun, loaded.
Dawn: There was. A boy in form five wanted to shoot this other boy so he brought a gun to school.

Are you kidding me?
Dawn: No. On my life – it's true.
Jamie: In our school.
Dawn: In our school, if you don't like someone you shoot 'em see. A boy hit a girl yesterday, and there was fighting.

Do you have sex education in your school?
Dawn: I have the most 'cause they are too young.

When does it start?
Dawn: Form four, age fourteen.

Sex, what do you think about it?
Natalie: I'm a virgin.
Dawn: She is. She's only twelve.

Drugs. What do you call drugs?
Dawn: Dope.

Apart from that, what do you call drugs?
Dawn: Disgusting.

Alcohol, is that a drug?
Dawn: No, it's an addiction.

Any drug can cause an addiction and alcohol is a drug. Do you call cigarettes a drug?
Natalie: Yes, and alcohol. Our friend Samantha, she got drunk once. So we made her drink coffee and gave her a biscuit. She snapped the biscuit – broke the biscuit – and she was so drunk....
Dawn: She wanted a funeral for the biscuit. So we had a funeral for the biscuit.
Jamie: Well, last Christmas I got so drunk I fell down the stairs.

Have you all been drunk?
ALL: Yes.
Natalie: I got drunk at a party – I couldn't walk up the hill.

How did you feel when you were drunk?
Natalie: I feel happier, I do.

Do you know anyone who uses dope?
Natalie: Yes, so and so does. We know 'cause of the people she goes around with.

Anyone tried to sell you anything at school?
Dawn: Yes. You know the youth club disco – well they was rolling joints and smoking them down

there. Anyone can smoke there.

Anything else?
Dawn: Pot, narcotics.
Natalie: I wouldn't buy nothing I wouldn't. Waste of money.

What music do you like?
Natalie: Pop, rave, Prince.
Dawn: They take ecstasy at raves.

What do you do after school?
Dawn: Get changed. Tease the jazz band.

Why?
Dawn: 'Cause they wear lamp shades on their heads. I used to play in the jazz band – on the mace – but I've finished. It's like a prison down there. Two hours down there – boring.

Are they very strict?
Dawn: Yes, and Jane shouts 'get in rank' – she don't know what she's doing.
Jamie: She's a crim.

What is a crim?
Jamie: Criminal. You know, the one who shouts? Well her son is in prison.

That doesn't make her a criminal.
Jamie: She's nasty.
Dawn: Her son pinches cars and stuff like that. And he does drugs in the house – mushrooms.
Sian: He pinched my mother's car three times.

That brings me to the vigilantes.
Dawn: They are not vigilantes. They're Village Action.
Jamie: They are called the Village Action Group and they are going round protecting people's cars.
Sian: Jane said the vigilantes smashed her windows. But the glass was on the outside. Now, does that make any sense?
Jamie: And they are supposed to have found a stone with a note attached to it.
Sian: She wrote on the window, on a piece of cardboard – 'Vigilantes did this'.
Jamie: And it's been there for a year. It was a year ago.
Dawn: And this is what she said to the news, or whatever. There was a stone with a piece of paper wrapped round it and it said on it – 'Remember, you've got a twelve year old daughter'.

You don't believe her?
Dawn: Na.
Why not?
Dawn: She's the biggest buller in the game.
Jamie: We've got a councillor up here right? LAUGHS
Natalie: This councillor got caught nicking.
Sian: And he had £230 in cash in his pocket. And he said, 'Oh, I forgot to put it in my trolley'. He put it straight in his bag.
Sian: And the Reverend Waggett stuck up for him.
Dawn: The stupid Vicar wants to make the 'Western' into a church. He does – and he takes all the old people's pension off them.
Jamie: Loads of people have stopped going to

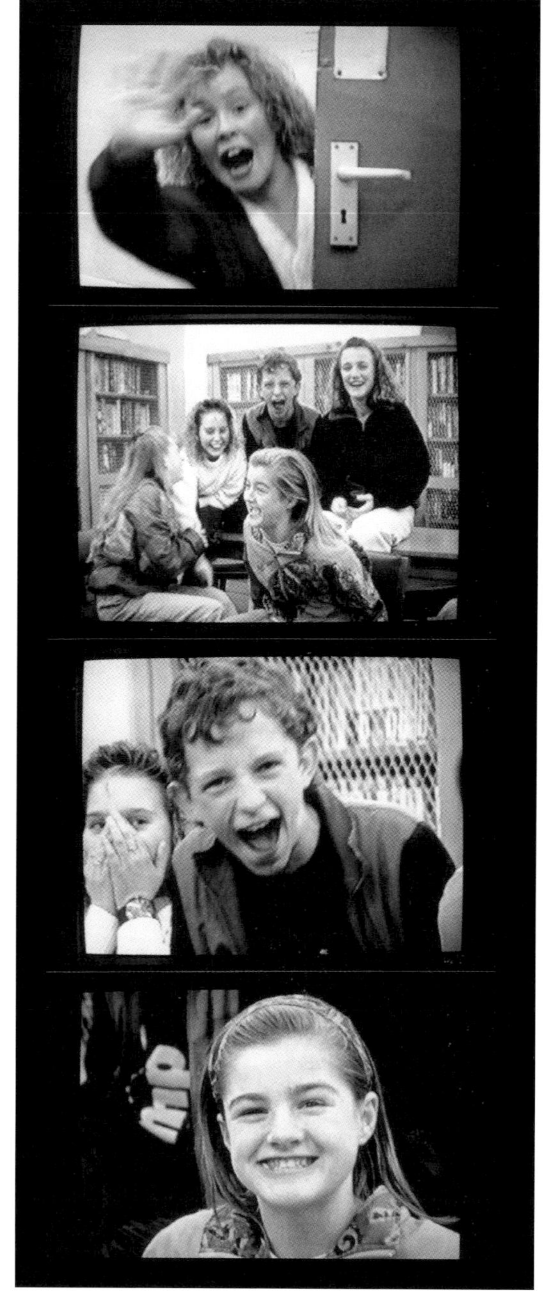

church now.

Dawn: My uncle Terence had cancer and Father Jeff thought he had cured him. But he didn't did he? He wears a leather jacket everywhere.

What are the good things about Aber and Blaengwynfi then?

Jamie: This hall used to be free, except for the snooker. Now we've got to pay loads to get in here. Nobody comes here now.

Dawn: There was the boy's club. Jane started that – she was taking money off us – subs like – and she wasn't even part of the Boy's Club Assocation.

What would be good up here?

ALL: A swimming pool.

Dawn: They knocked the flats down. They could put a pool down there.

What are you going to do when you leave school?

Sian: Be very, very lazy.

Natalie: Teach little children. I want to be a Welsh teacher.

Do you speak Welsh now?

Natalie: Yes. We do French too.

What do you like eating?

Dawn: Crisps, Nutella, chocolate.

Do you never think about your teeth?

Natalie: I've just had a filling in the front here.

Jamie: No

Do you eat fruit?

ALL: Yes – and curried nuts.

Where do you shop, locally?

Jamie: No, we go away – only crisps and things. There's Pakis in the shop across the road. They eat rice and things off little plates. Ugh.

What is wrong with that?

Jamie: And they eat a bit off an apple and then put it back. The children sleep under the counter – have you seen that? Anyway the police have warned people not to get stuff from there.

Why not?

Jamie: He's supposed to have done it with a frozen chicken. LAUGHS

Anne Brain

One of eight founder members of the Gwynfi Housing Co-op – the only one of its kind in Wales

The co-op was mainly set up to have better housing 'cause where we was living (Park Lane Flats) there was a lot of damp problems, problems with rats, problems of vandalism 'cause people were coming in and writing all over the passage-ways. People from the flats was having the blame for it and it wasn't them that was doing it – it was people from outside. The Council was blaming us for it. There were a lot of structural problems with the flats and terrible condensation. They had steel windows. Some of the flats were all right, they never had no problems, but others had terrible damp. They were only thirty years old when they bulldozed them.

It started a few years ago with the Octavia Trust. They wanted to buy the flats and do them up but that fell through. Then, one day I had a letter off John Greyland. Well, I didn't know who he was, so I rang him up and arranged a meeting. Well, unfortunately, I forgot about the first meeting but he didn't write only to me – he wrote to a few other people and they went to the first meeting and told me about the next meeting then – and I've been going to them ever since.

Shelter had been coming up the flats for a number of years when people were having problems with their housing. John Greyland contacted Shelter because they were looking for some people to set up a co-operative type of thing – and they thought of us.

As a community we got on all right. There was always someone around if you needed help. We was close. We had our problems – a few quarrels – but the flats were not fit to live in.

The first thing we had to do was get the land. John had already looked into the problem – what we could have – and he suggested this bit of land but we were told to look for another site as well, just in case. So we had a look at another site but I don't think it would have been very suitable anyway because it was originally houses on it anyway. But the council was very good about it because they, more or less, wanted us off their books anyway. They actually bought the land for us but we had to pay a nominal fee of £10. It was classified for industrial use but nobody would build a factory up here.

There was the river one side and the railway the other but they stopped the railway coming up here, filled in the tunnel that went through to the Rhondda and landscaped it. So we had to have loads of tests done to make sure that the ground was safe to build on. The road is built on the old railway line now, but the houses are built on the land that was actually there. We had a few arguments about this in the Committee but I think I won in the end – once they saw the old photographs.

I was living in the flats for seventeen years and I'm still finding it a bit strange – waking up in the morning and wondering where I am. But the new houses are lovely – lovely and warm. In the flats, whatever time of year it was, you'd freeze; you'd have to have a fire – in here now it's lovely and warm. The bedrooms, in the flats, you'd freeze. Even in the summer, if there was a heatwave they was always cold – as if someone had died in them – you know what I mean? Like a ghost was in them. All the flats, no matter what condition they was in, the bedrooms were always cold. But in these houses you can't breathe 'cause they are so warm.

We've got direct access to the road now, whereas before, up the flats, if it snowed you were snowed in. The gritter wouldn't go up there. But being on the road, by here now, they've got to keep the main road clear haven't they?

From start to finish, to get these houses built, took four years. Until the first foundation stone went in people didn't believe it was going to happen. But when we dug our first piece of ground… people were saying they are not going to be built and this and that – and I kept saying they are – be going soon to sign the contracts – going up the Welsh Office to get the money….

Then I actually signed for the money, and it was a lot of money, one and a half million – we haven't actually seen the money – but it was there when we wanted it.

Ninety-nine percent of the people from the flats moved down here. A few were re-housed by the Council. Our priority is families. There's ten two-bedroomed houses, seventeen three-bed-roomed and four one-bedroomed flats. The Co-op owns the properties and the freehold of the land. We had a say in the planning – we told the architect what we wanted. He did the drawings, fetched them back and what we didn't like – we changed. He tried to make us change our minds on a few things but we told him – no. We didn't want them and had what we wanted. There were some things, because of Building Regulations, we couldn't have.

We had a say in exactly what colour we wanted the rooms. They told us there were three basic colours we could have. We said we wanted another colour added and they thought it was strange but when they did a survey over fifty percent wanted this certain colour. So they added it in. I think we made them change their minds about their basic colour scheme for houses!

The Co-op is now a registered housing association with the Swansea Housing Association as managing agent. It is run by its own elected management committee of fifteen people. The majority are the actual tenants but one or two are co-opted in. We do get our problems – we have our arguments – different things – the number of dogs people are allowed to have for instance. In the houses, they are allowed to have two dogs per

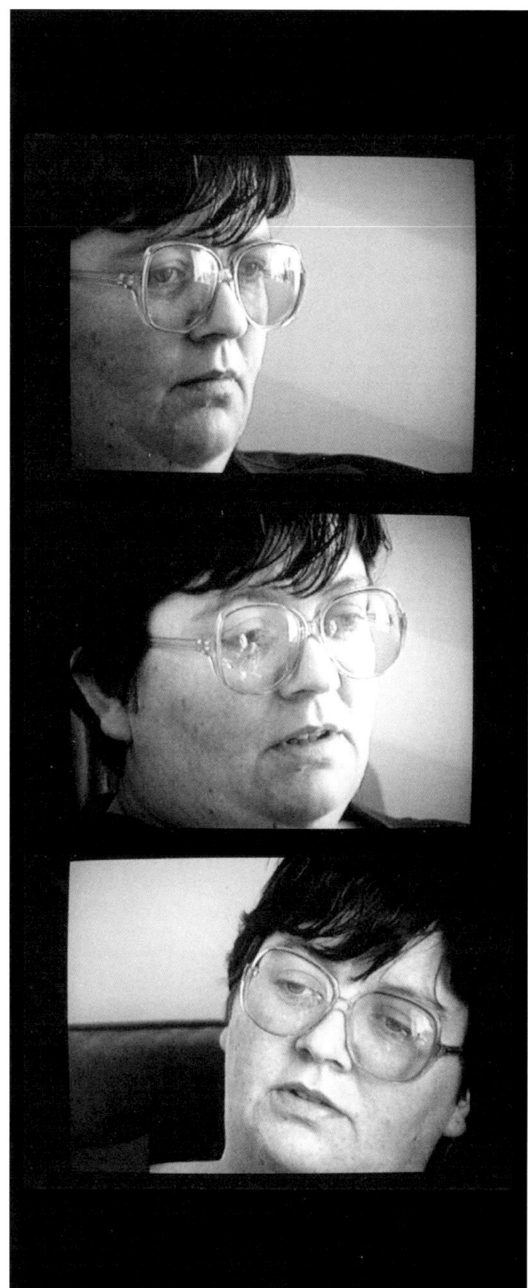

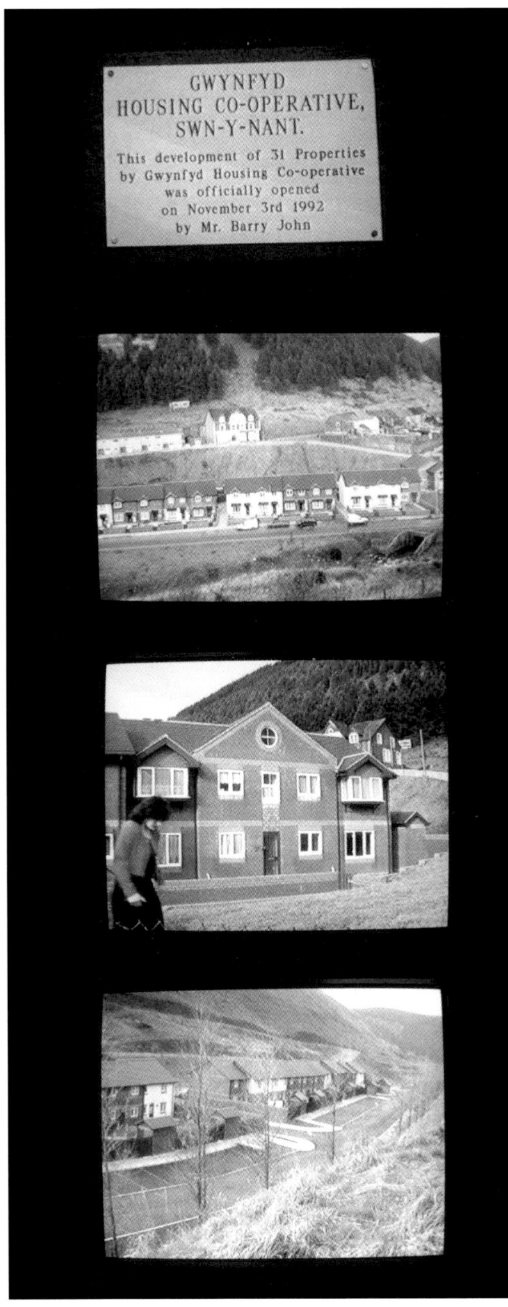

dwelling, but in the flats they can only keep one. We would like for them not to have no dogs but it's not fair on some of the tenants because they like animals. Only one tenant in the flats actually got a dog – the others don't want to bother – but he only got it because he's had it for years.

The main problems are over allocating. Whether some people should have them or not but you go by the majority – they have a vote on it and that's that. Anybody can have an application form. We have a point system – the person that's more desperate will have it. But we don't have a big turnover of houses – we wish we had more but we could only build what was allocated.

The biggest cost was met by a grant from Tai Cymru but we still had to have a mortgage. This is a problem at the moment. We are paying Tai Cymru but we are supposed to satisfy a bank or building society that we can run our own finances before they will give us a mortgage. But things are looking up. We have to pay off £700,000 and also set aside money for repairs, administration costs and one hundred and one little things that crop up. At the moment we are still under guarantee but after the year is up we got to administer the repairs as well.

The closeness is not as warm now as it used to be up the flats. Perhaps it's because now they've got their own homes, their own front door. Like when we was livng in the flats we only had one front door didn't we? Everybody had to use that. We was all on top of one another. They still go into each other's houses – some people don't bother as much as they used to but they all come back to you in the end – they all come round for a cup of coffee eventually.

Some have done a lot to their gardens and others haven't. Some have managed to get the money to do it but others not. We all want to have nice gardens but the ground isn't a hundred percent so... Most people know exactly what they want but it's having the money to do it. Ninety-nine percent are on Income Support. They're not working and can't really afford to do it. But they can sit outside in their gardens now whereas we couldn't sit out very much in the flats 'cause there was nowhere really for us to sit.

Swansea Housing have done a lot of training with us. Tai Cymru have paid for us to have training from a London Co-op who came down here to do the training. Every one of us can have the training – in fact the people who came down from London were very surprised by the turnout 'cause we had sixty percent there. It was even people who weren't on the Management Committee who turned out for the training sessions. Well, the London people were very surprised. The tenants want to get more involved but they don't want to do it without training of some sort. The training has made us see some of the problems and how to deal with them because it's not an easy thing to do. There is a lot of hard work so unless you are prepared to make a commitment – it's not like you can just put in a couple of weeks – you got to be committed to do it and really mean it. Not 'I've done my bit and I'm not going to do no more.' You got to be prepared to understand it. It's a lot easier than people think, but you got to have the training and it's a lot of hard work. Then, all of a sudden, everything clicks in together and you can actually explain it to others. To get to that point you've got to have the training. If there's anything we can't understand we've got

Swansea to fall back on and they can help us.

The houses are £58 per week – you can't charge the same for a flat – the flats are £41. They started out at a lower price but with inflation, last April we had to put the rents up. People say that's awful expensive, but there are houses that have been refurbished up here and they are charging almost as much for a refurbished house as for a new house.

We had the park area put in for the children – we've got forty-seven under thirteen – and the cost of that is being met by the Co-op itself – nothing to do with the Council. We wanted a safe area for the children to play. Being on the main road is a bit dangerous. Some people didn't like it mind – not people from here – some people don't like the idea of a park being there. But I say, would you rather have the children playing in the road? We have had a problem with the street behind because they wasn't happy about these houses being built in the first place. Some say we took their view away but it's not much of a view – of a road? Because of the state of the old flats, everybody was tarred with the same brush. But everybody's not the same.

Whereas we've been trying to improve ourselves, they think we are going to end up like the flats was – very prejudiced – there's a lot of prejudices against us – any little fault. You get one or two making complaints – but sometimes it's not actually our fault. How do you stop somebody riding up and down on a motor-bike – someone who doesn't live here – without getting the Police involved?

We had trouble with the vigilantes throwing stones through windows and we got problems with boys who are actually stealing cars and driving them into the car park. Young boys, they can be anything between fourteen and twenty years of age. The vigilantes set up because of the boys stealing cars and setting them on fire. One particular boy runs a driving school, that's his business. He also has a newsagents, but driving instructor, that's his main thing. Well, he kept having his car stolen – within a few months he had three cars nicked. Well, the insurance company are not going to keep paying out all the time and not only that, he was losing business wasn't he? It wasn't only him. A few other boys round here had their cars stolen. They didn't only take them and was joy-riding, they'd take them and burn them. Well, if you've got a car and you've paid a good few thousand pounds for it….. to have it stolen, smashed up, ripped to pieces and then burned… it is wrong. The boys are in the wrong for stealing the cars in the first place but the vigilantes are in the wrong for taking the law into their own hands. So I don't agree with either side.

The Police do patrol round here but they have changed some of them 'cause people have been victimised. I think somebody is going to get hurt who is nothing to do with either the vigilantes or stealing; somebody's going to get killed and then there'll be a war up here. They'd be round and they wouldn't care whose property they're smashing up – the boys who stole the cars, the Neighbourhood Watch – they call it. Somebody is going to get hurt and then they'll be running riots round here. Some of the boys are just going round in cars reporting things but others are going round with baseball bats, beating people up. It's the parents I feel sorry for. How can you keep an eighteen year old boy under control? You can't be with him twenty-four hours a day.

If the parents are stricter when they are younger, the boys would learn to understand right from wrong, but if they get away with murder when they are young, they are going to do it when they are older. One of the boys now, he got lovely parents. They tried all they can to help him but he just doesn't want to know. I think they just do it to have a buzz. If they are not stealing cars they are into drugs – you name it they can get it – and they are breaking into people's houses to get the money for drugs. We've had several break-ins down here. You are talking about eight or ten boys, at the most, hanging round here – some of them are related to the tenants. But what are you going to do? We can't actually say 'Well, you've got to get out 'cause you're related to so and so and they are causing problems.' You can choose your friends but you can't choose your family if you know what I mean.

It's a buzz and a lot of boredom. They are unemployed. They are trying to get jobs or they are on these schemes. They are going but they are not doing anything, just sitting around all day – bored. They are bored in work, they come home and they are still bored so they either take it out on their family or they go out and cause problems. And they're not getting enough money – that's why they are stealing. What do they get on a YTS scheme, £27 a week? And some of them have got to travel to Neath. Their parents help them out but they aren't better off. This is another problem we got. The parents are sick of supporting them – they are quarrelling and throwing the boys out on the road so they are looking for somewhere to sleep and they get into trouble that way.

They go the Social Security, the council and they can't help them 'cause they haven't got the properties to put them in. There was talk about turning the Park Lane Flats into homes for single people but they was in such a bad state.... As soon as we were moving out of them they were breaking into them and stealing all the pipes – the copper. There was one, she hadn't moved out a half hour and they were in there and vandalised it. They kicked the door in and ripped out all the copper, the tanks – anything worth money.

We had a break-in down here. They stole the fire out of one the houses. We know who done it but we didn't have any actual proof. And we've been told this – he sold a £600 fire for thirty quid just to have money for drugs. Since we've been here we've had a lot of vandalism ourselves. Everywhere in the village people are getting broke into so this Neighbourhood Scheme isn't working very well is it?

The Government should try to get proper jobs not just working on schemes where you get ten pound on top of your dole 'cause that's nothing. By the time they pay their bus fares out of that – and they are sitting around on top of that. They are on about not having enough qualified people – well – when youngsters go there the employers are not taking the time to train them. How can they get qualifications that way? They are giving early retirement these days – you can't win either way. You are either too young or you are too old for it. People who want to work can't get the jobs 'cause they're too young and haven't got the skills or they are too old for it.

We've been asked will we be building any more houses – well we don't know. At the moment we are very dependent on Swansea Housing. We don't know if we will be able to go on our own – that is what we have to find out over the next five years. But the main thing is having the confidence. If you got the confidence you can do what you like – you can achieve what you like. We've achieved a lot getting the houses built and we've met a lot of people. People like the Lord Mayor and going to Cardiff and talking to a lot of people about finances. When we first started off – there are only three of the original committee left – we met a lot of people, but the people who are coming in now haven't actually met what we call the big noises and got the confidence to do a lot of the things we have done. This means that they have got to get the skills and the training over the years. Whether I'll stay on the committee I don't know. I might leave and come back to it but I'm always there if they want help and advice – even if I'm not on the committee. I haven't actually made up my mind but the only way they'll get me out of this house is in a wooden box. I've worked too hard and too long to give it up.

The committee have worked hard, not only me and Sandra. Now it's up to the new members to learn how to tell other people what to do. They've got to be prepared to listen, to compromise, whether they like it or not. Everyone works together, everyone has to compromise. Some people will like it and others won't. I'm praying that everything will work together and in five, perhaps ten, years people will want to build more

houses – everyone would know then what they are doing. It's like doing a job – you got to stick with it – go on holiday, have a break, but come back to it – don't give in.

If they vote against you well, that's tough luck. In the end it will always come back to the truth. If you are wrong – then admit it. If you are right, you can smirk about it but they got to admit that they were wrong. That's what co-operation means.

Swansea have been marvellous with us. They are with us for the next five years – we've got that back-up. They want us to succeed. They've learned from us – we have given them ideas. We are actually the first co-operative in Wales to start from the beginning – from scratch, so we are hoping that everything will work out and that then there could be more similar co-ops in Wales. If you get one or two people that are prepared to work you can motivate others. But you got to keep that motivation going or everything will fall apart. Now our work is actually starting. We can't sit back – there's a long way to go yet.

After a year, when the guarantee runs out, then the houses are our responsibility. I don't think some of the committee have realised that. At the moment our responsibility is to keep the tenants in line – to keep their houses tidy – that they don't upset the neighbours around. Like when we was with the council – if you had a complaint you went to the council and they would sort it out. But if a neighbour makes a complaint here then it is the committee that has to go and sort it out – we try and sort it out. If we can't we call Swansea in and they mediate. We can't throw anybody out though, it isn't as easy as that.

Geraint & Andrew

Residents of Gwynfyd Housing Association

Are you living in the new houses?
Yes.

How do you like it?
Good.

What is good about it?
G: There's big gardens in there. They're warm…. And bigger compared with the flats.

You lived in the flats. What's different down here?
A: No rats down here.

You go to school, like it?
G: Yes, we have swimming and rugby we do, and football and stuff.

You are playing football here?
G: I'm learning him I am.
A: I'm training for going up the top school. I got one year.
G: I'm learning him for when he's up the top school.
A: That's my school, up above the flats and that's his school, up above mine.
G: Know the Western? Up there, up above that.

What do you want to be when you grow up?
G: Fireman.
A: Footballer.

So you are going to work hard.
G: It's learning him that's all I am. He don't know.

What do you have for breakfast?
A: Branflakes, Weetabix.
G: Cornflakes, Weetabix, Rice Krispies and all that I do have.

What do you do after breakfast when you haven't got school?
G: Get dressed and feed my ferrets.

You have ferrets, where, up the wood?
G: In my back garden.

Have you any other pets?
A: Mine's died. Choked on a dog biscuit.

What was he?
G: Jack Russell.

So when you've fed your ferrets, what do you do then?
G: Go out playing football and then we go hunting with my father, down Pontrhydyfen.

What do you hunt?
G: Rabbits.
A: And I go hunting with my uncle as well.

Do you take the ferret?
G: His uncle, my father and his father goes together.

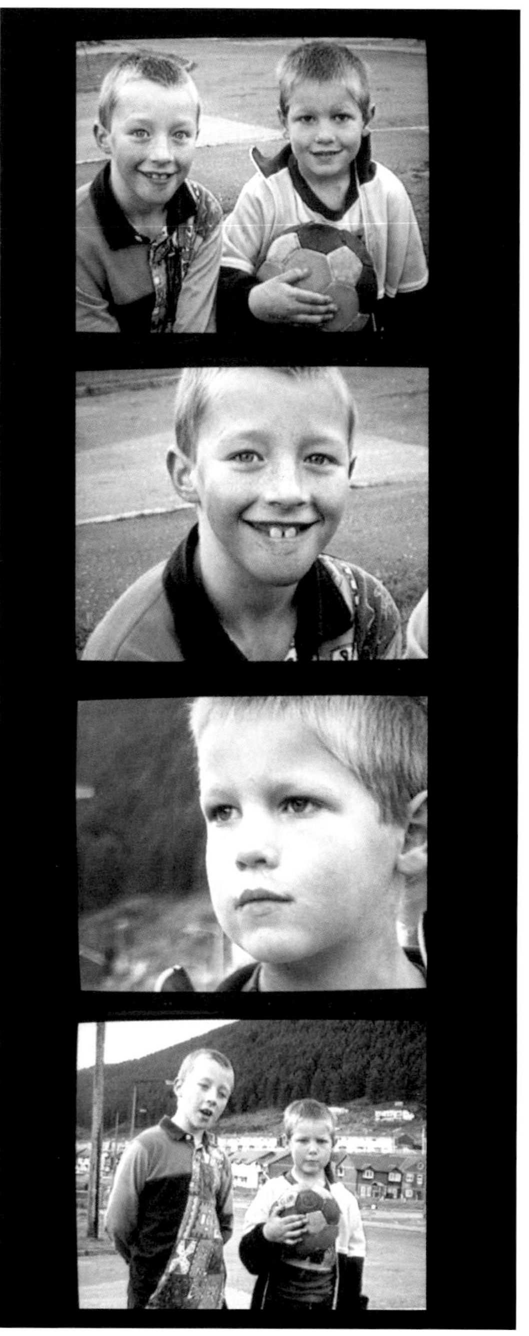

Do you catch many?

G: Eight or nine a week.

That keeps you in food?

G: It does, a bit.

What else do you like doing?

G: Fishing down Forest Lodge.

A: And I go fishing down a big cliff with my father.

How old are you, Andrew?

A: Six, seven in two weeks.

What do you want for your birthday?

G: He's hoping a fishing rod off his father and a lamp off my mother.

A: And I'm having a clock off my mother.

How old are you, Geraint?

G: Nine.

Listen you two, if you were a politician, know what a politician is?

G: No.

Someone who decides things, has a lot of power. If you were one and you had a lot of money and you wanted to give it to the valley, what would you do with it? Think hard.

G: Give it to the poor.

A: Buy proper food.

What makes you happy?

A: Going fishing.

Futures

Tina Carr & Annemarie Schöne

The valleys of South Wales were mined for coal for little more than a single century. Not a vast amount of time in terms of history but long enough to transmogrify the entire landscape from one of agricultural green to another of industrial black. Smooth, rolling hills and vales were transformed by the creation of conical spoil heaps, table-mountains of slag, chimneys, flues, aerial ropeways and pit-head winding gear, not to mention the rows upon rows of two up and two down miners' cottages dug into and clinging on to the steep valley sides. The environmental damage was, and remains, immense. The air, the water and the earth rapidly became polluted, as did the miners' lungs by the 'dust' they were enveloped in every day of their working lives. These facts were recklessly ignored by all and sundry for the best part of the so-called industrial era. Industrialisation was seen as pro-gress, 'scientific' – just as 'the new technology', computers and a multi-media virtual reality are viewed today.

Miners were connected, not only to each other, but also to the earth in what can only be described as a spiritual way. United in common cause with one another and locked in battle with nature, extracting her minerals but also reverencing her, 'tributing' her in their lives above ground. Often the miner, after a shift below ground, in semi-darkness, subject to sensory deprivation, would come up and fly his pigeons or dig in his allotment, drawing fresh breath in gratitude for his continued survival. Women and children joined in this fight for survival by necessity and to the utmost in ways that have become legendary, especially in times of extreme hardship such as strikes or wars.

All who were born into it have the distinct feeling that the mining landscape is home. The physical environment influenced their spirit and soul just as the substances and forces taken in with the dust they swallowed and food they ate made their developing physical bodies part of the soil of the valleys. As bearer of the physical senses, the body is an instrument of the soul, so that from the earliest days a basic configuration of inner experience develops against the background of the miner's landscape both above and below ground. Thus we see a reflection of the light and darkness in the basic inner mood of the miner, something that comes to full expression in all aspects of the culture of mining communities. The nature of the soil, in its wider sense, is reflected in the inner and outer configuration of the people. The basic temperament is characteristic of the whole community. It is an identity that becomes the elemental force of homesickness for people who leave, or are forced to leave, the soil they have come to love; a destiny hundreds of thousands of miners and their families have had to live through in the past thirty years.

The landscape puts its imprint on the body and soul of its inhabitants. On the other hand, the human spirit, soul and body through work puts its imprint on the environment. Unfortunately, our age destroys community, undermines folk traditions, makes people homeless and strangers to the landscapes in which they live. Genuine, unadulterated folk traditions are hardly to be found any more and yet only three decades ago, horses still pulled the plough just as they pulled the coal drams in the pits. When it was ploughing, harrowing, sowing or harvesting time, the whole village worked as the cycles of nature demanded, thus creating a common cause and a spiritual frame-work. A regular rhythm was observed, with everyone starting early in the morning and finishing when evening came, all of it with hardly a word spoken, at a measured pace and free from haste. One could literally feel the power of the rural tradition that supported people and created community. Out of this wholeness, a certain attitude to the inner life of nature would arise in the daily work, for instance in the way the soil would be worked, plants and animals looked after. Every folk tradition thus created its own image in working with nature and these images are the cultivated landscapes which we see all around us today.

Mining was a comparable, albeit industrial, tradition based on work skills, a very particular knowledge and expertise with the distinction that it visually despoiled the landscape rather more obviously than agricultural methods whose destructiveness is as insidious although largely invisible to the eye (pesticides, nitrates etc.).

Efforts are being made to renaturalise mining areas, remove offending spoil heaps and remodel the landscape; not always with a great deal of success, as in the case of the Upper Afan Valley, because the problem needs to be addressed holistically and not piecemeal.

The area should be prioritised, the political will and the resources mustered and the communities engaged, such as happened in the Ruhr area of Germany forty years ago when their coal mining ceased. Green Action, the Communal Association of the Ruhr Area (KVR Ruhrgebiet) and Ruhrkohle AG (the German equivalent of the National Coal Board/British Coal) got together and decided to renaturalise the whole area of the Ruhr Coalfield, with its population centres of Essen, Bochum and Duisburg, with the idea of providing leisure areas where formerly mining had been. The result was a quick green area for fourteen million people in the Ruhr, considered, designed and executed with typical German precision and forward thinking. All the pithead winding gear were preserved in situ as monuments to the industry – the largest becoming the symbol of the vast German Mining Museum at Bochum – as was the network of lakes, canals and waterways. The spoil heaps were re-modelled from unstable conical and table-mountain shapes to those more natural looking, and a small amount of topsoil was added. The whole area was then re-seeded with wild flowers, grass mixture, lupin and clover to create humus where formerly there was none. Areas were designated for specific planting depending upon their position and soil constitution – whether it was rocky or flammable. Indigenous pioneer trees, such as birch, and shrubs were then planted to create a stable plant community. The agricultural uses were ascertained and grain and potatoes grown with considerable and continued success. Vines were planted on the black sides of spoil heaps – because these were shown to absorb and retain heat – producing a wine with a very special flavour. And last but by no means least, the nature reserve aspect was considered whereby naturalisation was allowed to occur without interference or assistance. The whole was then networked with cycle tracks and walks and opened up for the general leisure and enjoyment of all. Cycling through it today, it is hard to believe that this was one of the most heavily industrialised, heavily polluted areas in the whole of Europe only forty years ago.

This example speaks volumes for the regenerative powers of plants, and the importance of the part all plants play in the life cycle of not just small areas like the Ruhr or Upper Afan Valley, but our planet as a whole.

A plethora of environmental crises – global warming, loss of biodiversity, tropical deforestation – is at their core, issues involving plants. The peoples of the earth have long depended upon plants for food, clothing, shelter, energy (wood, charcoal, coal, oil), transportation, medicine and ritual. Plants are able to transform atmospheric gases and minute quantities of inorganic nutrients into life itself, whereas animals (including people) depend on consumption not only for their lives but also for the way they live. It is the food animals eat that determines their position in the ecological community; plants are vast factories of chemical diversity distinguished not by what they consume but by what they produce – literally from thin air. The photosynthetic pathway leading from carbon dioxide to wood means that the massive rain-forests of the Amazon have ultimately been pro-duced from thin air (carbon dioxide and sunlight) whilst simultaneously releasing life-giving oxygen into the atmosphere.

Up to fifty per cent of all living things – at least five million species – are estimated to live in tropical forests. The unparalleled diversity of species within these forests means relatively few individuals of each; any forest clearance thus disrupts their life cycles and threatens them with rapid extinction. Current estimates suggest that we are losing one species of life a day from the five to ten million species believed to exist.

Small, sustainable societies (tribal) provide us with models, living examples of communities that live in harmony with nature, their environment and each other; based not on exploitation and the economics of the stock market but on networks of kinship and trading only for one's real needs. Societies in which 'a poor man shames us all' rather than ours in which the Pharisee passes by on the other side of the road; that is if he acknowledges the existence of poverty in our country in the first place.

In 1973 Dr Schumacher, interestingly, Economic Advisor to the National Coal Board from 1950 to 1970, wrote *Small Is Beautiful*, which looked at the economic structure of the western world in a 'revolutionary way'. He maintained that man's current pursuit of profit and progress, which promotes giant organisations and increased specialisation, has in fact resulted in gross economic inefficiency, environmental pollution and inhumane working conditions. He challenges the doctrine of economic, technological and scientific specialisation and proposes a system based on much smaller working units, communal ownership and regional workplaces utilising local labour and resources. With the emphasis on the person not the product, *Small Is Beautiful* points the way to a world in which capital serves man instead of man remaining a slave to capital. Schumacher's words have been often quoted and his theories reiterated and rehashed ever since – he must be turning in his grave – since so little of his wisdom has been put into practice.

Schumacher's theory could be achieved though – easily – and especially in places like Upper Afan where, with a little bit of imagination, the desertified wasteland of landscape left in the wake of coal mining, could be transformed into viable, productive units of place and people. A re-greening of the environment, similar to the Ruhr project, would be a good starting point. The growth and utilisation of indigenous plants such as leeks, whinberries, soft fruit, flowers could be turned into commercial propositions run by local people. The skills necessary are undoubtedly there – one only has to look at all the tidy allotments and gardens in the valley to realise that, and the possibilities are endless and sustaining.

Plants and their uses are myriad. Cotton, hemp and flax provide fibre for clothes, paper and rope and a plant such as wode (*Estasis tincoria*), which, along with hemp, will proliferate weed-like on even the poorest of soils, has a half a dozen other uses apart from the well-known blue dye that is extracted from it. Wode can also be used as a wood preserver, a paint, a paper conservator and textile powder. It is primarily an environmentally friendly base to which can be added other colour providers. It can be used in the renovation of old buildings since it has similar properties to lime wash. Wode straw is also used as an insulation material or can be turned into alcohol. Eight by-products could be manufactured locally from the commercial production of just one plant.

Plants grown for their medicinal properties would also have a number of uses as teas, tinctures, tablets, ointments, soaps, shampoos and these could include most of our very common herbs such as thyme, sage, rosemary, marigold, Vervain (an ancient Welsh herb) or evening primrose. Organic market gardening growing indigenous herbs, vegetables and trees is just as viable an idea as three boating lakes stocked with a few fish that provide one or two jobs and that most of the local population cannot make use of, because they have no interest in fishing or it is beyond their means.

There seems little doubt that the Ponds Project was a cosmetic exercise born out of local politics, a quick result, so that something (it could have been anything really) was seen to be done about the plight of a deprived community in need of everything. The Ponds are simply representational of money having been spent – a slap in the face for every member of that community. The politicians and local councillors are now off the hook because they can point at a pond and say that they have created a facility to which tourists and their loads of money will be attracted.

But not one valley man got a proper job out of it and the whole community was derided in the Swansea paper for lacking skills. No wonder they were bitter about it. No one bothered to enquire what skills did and do exist within the communities of the Upper Afan Valley. No one asked the people, the valley residents, what, in their opinions, would benefit the valley in terms of their needs and desires if proper jobs could not be created overnight. What would make life easier for them, for example better public transport, more amenities (considering the quantity they have lost in the past twenty years), and a swimming pool perhaps for the large numbers of children hanging around on street corners.

Attract tourists by all means, but don't try to pretend that mining didn't exist in this valley. The communities are proud of their heritage, proud to be part of the industrial heartland of South Wales. They want their roots acknowledged, saluted and a future excavated from a past that remains well within living memory.

The frequency of natural and industrial disasters

(Bhopal, Chernobyl), popular global protests and brave direct action by publicly supported environmental agencies throughout the world have given rise to a growing awareness among more and more people of facts and figures that reveal the enormity and consequence of the criminal degradation inflicted on land, water and air. Such awareness is questioning and opposing the sanctity of continued economic and industrial growth and scientific advance, at those punishing costs to our common habitat. This awareness lays bare also that such growth for its own sake is plainly dangerous and leads to deformity in the natural world which can only hold its equilibrium to a limited extent. Moreover, this awakening points to the fact that it is not a universally accepted formula for progress or even a so-called category, but the special project of a highly organised, elite grouping, socially and technologically bent on holding and increasing its power, influence and wealth.

This World Wide Web links business tycoons, drug barons, billionaires, millionaires, family clans, organised crime (Mafia), monarchs and despotic rulers, corrupt governments and weak politicians, industrial and insurance companies, vast multinationals and their shareholders, landowners and holders, world bankers and traders. It possesses and manoeuvres huge and diverse investments in industries such as mining (coal, metal), quarrying (stone, cement), drilling (oil, gas), agriculture, building and communication. Financial interests and capital globally control the mass production, mass processing, mass distribution and amassing of all our

material goods such as food (from grain to beef), our drink (from water and milk to beer and Coke), our clothes, shoes and cosmetics (from jeans to perfume), our drugs (from aspirin to heroin and tobacco), our arms and cars and planes, fuels, electronics, computers….

Simultaneously, big business also lusts for complete control of our entire public and private entertainment, leisure, social life, spiritual beliefs and cultures, language, music, art and the enormous pecuniary profits growing thereof. For that very reason it needs to invade our own personal sphere, our character, substance and spiritual freedoms necessary to experience and express, through all our senses, our soul, our mind. The information essential to our process of self realisation, growth and development needs to be received from and transmitted through daily physical, sensual, emotional and cognitive contact and intercommunication with the natural world full of an infinite abundance of people and other life forms. Such interaction gives us our sense of reality, the feeling of being alive and a vital part of community and nature and thus the possibility, if we are lucky, strong and courageous, of becoming independent, knowledgeable, loving and creative selves.

Over the past few decades our very own private realities and the multitudinous variety of single experiences derived from them have been under accelerated attack. They have been (and are continuously being) subversively yet blatantly replaced with the ghost pictures and phantom figures emerging from a reality of another kind, a reality virtually constructed by information

technology and its masters/slaves. Our thoughts and ideas, our emotions, hopes and dreams, our material, mental and spiritual existence are cynically played with. They are systematically annihilated by concepts, sounds and images engineered by personalities other than our own in the service of industries seeking to promote particular products. These kinds of cultural chimeras flood the mass media and supermarkets, altering our minds, hearts and souls, inducing us to follow the competitive free market fluctuations of supply and demand.

The new age imperialists guarantee their profits using the age old method of exploitation. They keep labour cheap, having created the ideal conditions in which to do so, or they extinguish it altogether by introducing new technology. With financial clout they push high tech progress like a drug; its ideology has become yet another commodity to sell via the media super channels of propaganda.

Driven also by fear of the unknown (China, Islamic fundamentalism), this powerful elite globally spreads its omnipotent gospel of material affluence, preaches the moral credo of greed and thus incites the ethics of escalating violence in the full knowledge of national conflicts, spiritual uncertainty and utter economic deprivation among the majority of the world's population, which is faced with hopelessness, massive debts and ecological destruction.

In this context of status quo economic and military domination, natural science and research have been brought under the yoke of state and industry, rigidly fixed in the dogmas of capitalism and patriarchy both assumed by the institutions and executives of a political system calling itself democracy.

Huge funds are freed and administered to explore our outer and inner space in the almost desperate quest to attain Faustian knowledge in the desirable fields of electronics, biology, biochemistry, mathematics. Behind the aegis of advance lies the Moloch of conquest for gain.

De facto. Under such patronage high tech progress has become a synonym for the infamous and cruel endeavour to dematerialise and to despiritualise the world, to destroy life and to threaten the survival of our planet.

And so, these dire economic and environmental circumstances have made it our task – our duty, to change course and to oppose by refusing to take the bait of easy pre-packaged living, feeling and thinking. Resistance means to do without and to create alternative and independent ways to survive and to protest. We need to show courage, drive and hope, so that in the future we can find a balance between the ecological vulnerability of our world and the needs of the people that inhabit it.

TC & AS, 1996

Tina Carr & Annemarie Schöne

Tina Carr and Annemarie Schöne are two award-winning artists who work together on many diverse projects combining their skills of photography, video and design in innovative, socially conscious and environmentally friendly ways. They initiate and execute photographic projects, video installations and photo-sculptures which are exhibited internationally. They also design and build gardens, exterior features and public art. For more information visit www.simply-solar.co.uk.

Amanda Hopkinson

Amanda Hopkinson is a writer on photography and a literary translator. For ten years a Senior Research Fellow in Cardiff University's School of Journalism, Media and Cultural Studies, she is the present Director of the British Centre for Literary Translation at the University of East Anglia's School of Literature and Creative Writing.

Osi Rhys Osmond

Osi Rhys Osmond is from a Sirhowy Valley mining family, he is an artist, writer, teacher and broadcaster. He contributes regularly to magazines, including *Planet*, and is published extensively on the arts and culture in both Welsh and English. He has a longstanding and critically vigilant interest in depictions of the mining community.

Bronwen Colquhoun

Bronwen Colquhoun is Senior Curator of Photography at Amgueddfa Cymru – National Museum Wales. She curates the exhibitions programme for the Museum's permanent photography gallery and is responsible for the photography acquisitions programme within the Art department. She previously worked as Assistant Curator of Photographs at the Victoria and Albert Museum and holds a PhD from Newcastle University. At Amgueddfa Cymru Bronwen has curated exhibitions including *Swaps: Photographs from the David Hurn Collection*, *ARTIST ROOMS: August Sander*, *Bernd and Hilla Becher: Industrial Visions*, *The Sea Horizon: Garry Fabian Miller*, and *The Valleys*.

Acknowledgements

Tina & Annemarie would like to thank everyone who has participated in this project from its beginnings way back in 1990 (the mists of time) to the making of this book in 2008.

First and foremost, the video interviewees for their courage and humour.

The Arts Council of Wales, The Calouste Gulbenkian foundation, The Welsh Writers' Trust John Morgan Award.

Amanda Hopkinson and Osi Rhys Osmond for their perceptive and insightful contextualisation.

Gawain Davies (Gomer) for his care and attention to the digital scans of the 5 x 4 negatives.

Everyone at Parthian, especially Lucy Llewellyn, Jeff Teare, Alice Terry for her work on the DVD, Dominic Williams and Richard Davies.

We are immensely grateful to the National Screen and Sound Archive of Wales for their assistance in transferring the original Hi-8 material to mini DV. All the original tapes are in the Sound and Moving Image collection. Thank you to Iestyn Hughes and all the technical staff of the archive.

Special thanks to Sally & Gwil, Toria & Brian and Irma for their generous support over the years.

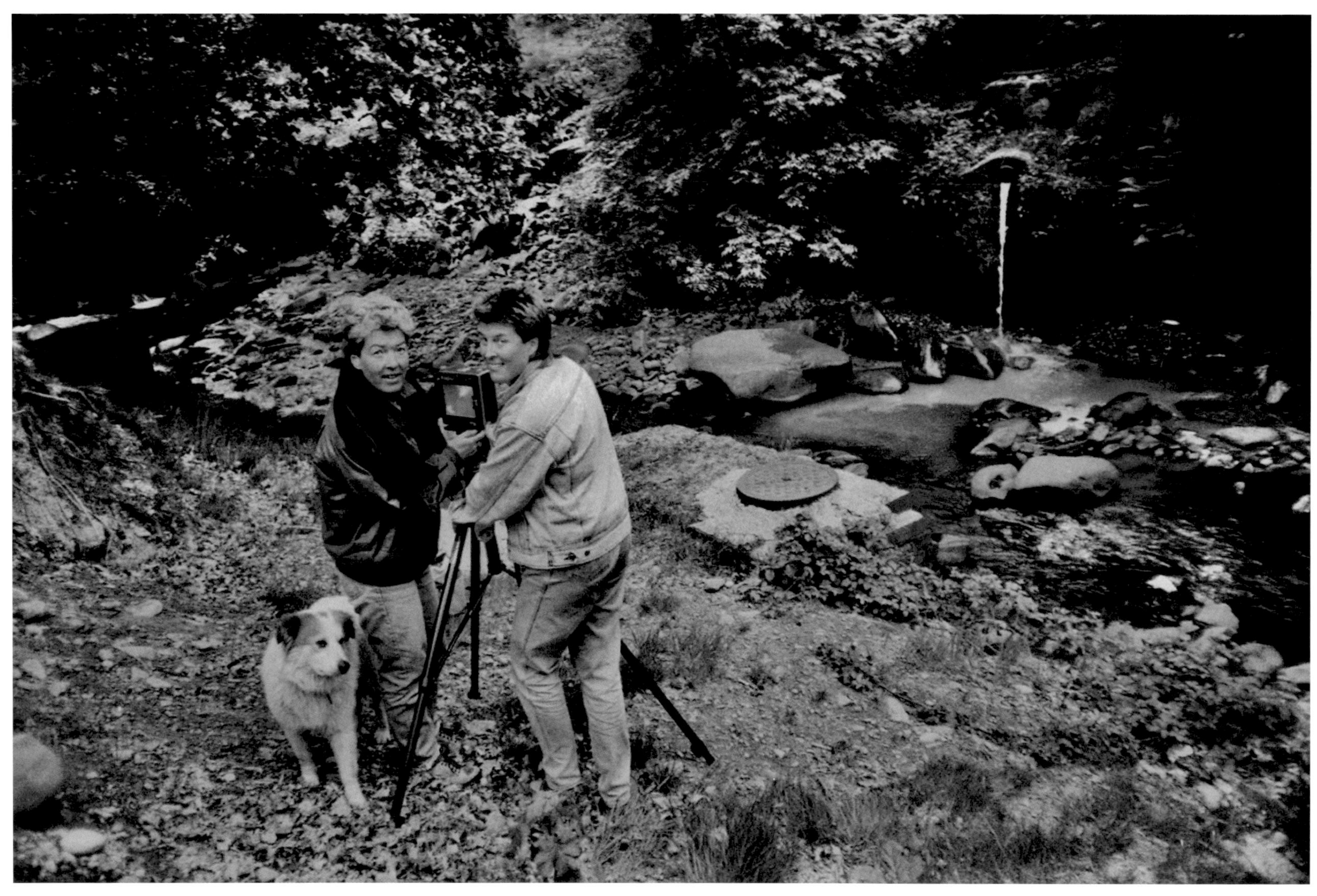

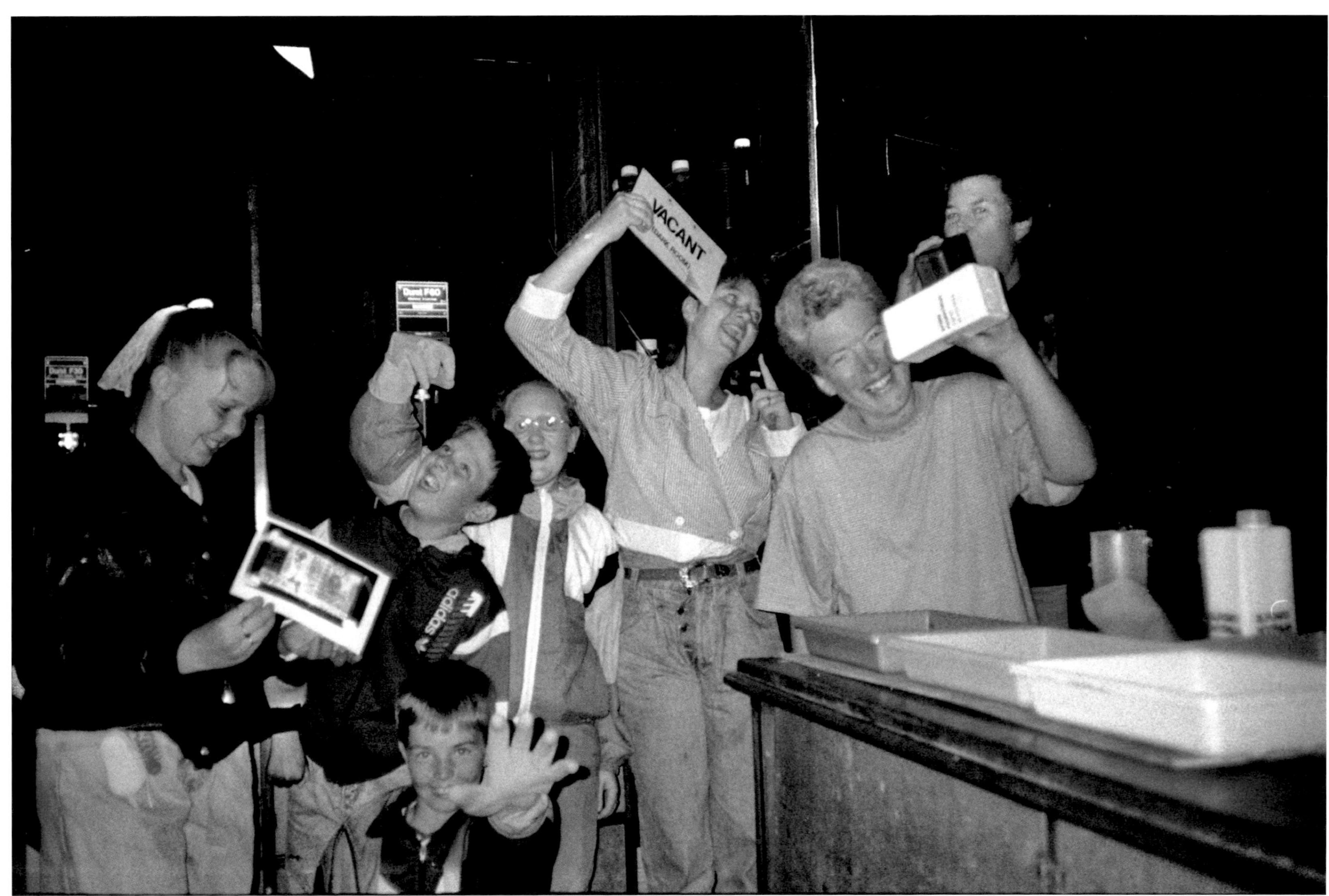